RINGMASTER

WORK, LIFE, AND KEEPING IT ALL TOGETHER

JENNIFER FOLSOM

ISBN: 978-1-6847-1432-2 (sc)
ISBN: 978-1-6847-1431-5 (e)

Library of Congress Control Number: 2019919738

Lulu Publishing Services rev. date: 12/17/2019

For Tia, for being my person

CONTENTS

INTRODUCTION

Working moms, I see you.

I see you ducking into the hallway out of your cube farm to take a call from your son's teacher, concerned about his inability to sit still at circle time. I see you lurking outside your daughter's recital, taking a call from a client angry about last week's messed-up invoice. There you are, hiding in a stairwell, holding back tears, after yet another morning argument with your spouse about who was doing what and when to get the family up and out to school and to work. Switching to mobile phone for a 4:00 p.m. concall so you can get your baseball prodigy to practice at 5:00 p.m. across town. Answering emails at 11:00 p.m to show your boss that your flexible schedule isn't slowing your team down, all the while cleaning the kitchen from tonight's dinner and baking tomorrow's Teacher Appreciation Breakfast banana bread. Because you aren't going to be one of *those* moms that stops at the Safeway bakery before kiss-and-ride. You're not going to be one of *those* professionals that lets her career slide while raising children.

This stuff is really hard. Contrary to popular belief, there is no work-life balance. If you are working and you have children, your life is a three-ring circus. And most of the books on the shelves today and the stories in your Google News feed are about that dizzying first year or two as a working parent: How to survive pumping. About finding the right daycare. How to transition back from maternity leave. But the real work-family conflict, it's a long-term problem, where the inputs and outputs change more frequently than most of us would like to admit. As it turns out, you will be working for a very long time and as I'm learning with teenagers, I am going to be parenting for the rest of my life. What you need is a framework for evaluating the daily — and sometimes hourly — decisions and trade-offs between your personal and professional lives.

And don't think for one second that I have all of the answers. Not by a long shot. I still duck into a bathroom stall to avoid crying at my desk. I am on my phone answering work emails when I should be engaging with my sons. But the difference is that I am out of the darkness with this and into the light. I am done hiding the struggle and the shame for not having it all figured out.

Time and again I turn for advice to the real-life working motherhood experts I see getting it done in my own life and work: The mom who was promoted to partner of an international law firm while working part-time. The neighbor who ran her own business while successfully launching four children into college. The single mom of three who still manages to get a hot, healthy meal on the table every night after an exhausting day at work. There are heroines among us every day, navigating the daily landmines of life and making it all work.

I hope reading this book encourages you to let yourself off the hook a little bit. To see that no one has this all figured out. That together, by lifting each other up, by sharing strategies and building our villages, we can successfully grow our careers and our families.

You are the RINGMASTER of your circus. You decide what goes in each ring: work, life, and you. You decide when and where the spotlight shines.

RING 1: WORK

The first ring in your three-ring circus is work. As a new working parent, your priorities may shift drastically. You won't be able to wait to leave until your boss leaves because your kids will need to be picked up, and if you don't make daycare pickup by 6:00 p.m., the provider will call Child Protective Services *and* charge you a ten-dollar-per-minute late fee.

As a working parent, you may care more about a telecommuting benefit than a prestigious title. You may choose to pass on a plum, promotion-worthy assignment because it requires 80 percent travel. Ultimately, once the little bosses enter the picture, your work view will be fundamentally different.

But what I've come to realize is that—in some form or fashion—you will continue to work for a very long time. And turns out, you will parent for the rest of your life. While most of the books on the "working mom's survival guide" bookshelf will focus on those first few years, you're going to need a framework for managing your work and life for a very long time.

As you likely transition from caring for young children to caring for aging parents or, God bless, are doing both at the same time, your view of work will shift throughout your career. As your life changes, so must your work.

Working when you have children is a circus, and there is no mythical "balance." But by leveraging specific career strategies, you can achieve some level of professional satisfaction and still get dinner on the table. In this section, I will walk you through each part of the job life cycle—from defining your new "dream job" through rocking the job you have—all in the context of working parenthood.

CHAPTER 1

DEFINING THE (WORK) RELATIONSHIP (DTWR)

Defining your priorities is the first step in finding any kind of sanity in your circus. While the twentysomethings spend their lunch hour gossiping about new relationships and whether they've had a DTR (define the relationship) or talked with the guy or gal they met on Bumble, as a working parent, you need to have a DTR with your work. You can't find a dream job—or something approximating it—without knowing specifically what you want.

As a partner in a flexible-role-focused staffing firm, I frequently met parents who would say, "I don't care what I do; I just need to be at the bus stop at 4:00 p.m." I get it. At many points in your life, being able to work around your children's schedule is important. But that's not a helpful answer, mostly because it's not true. You won't do just anything: you won't work for any price or in any location. In order for people to help you find your dream job, you first need to know what that is.

Whether it's a job-seeking parent with whom I'm working or a friend or colleague seeking advice, the most helpful thing I can hear is specifics of what he or she wants in a job. For example, I once worked with a candidate who knew exactly what she wanted and needed. She came to me and said, "I am open to any marketing, writing, communications, project management, or executive admin position in the, Northern Virginia area—Arlington, Falls Church, Alexandria. My ultimate goal is to find a permanent role working twenty to twenty-five hours per week, virtually or on-site, three to four days a week, between the hours of 9:30 a.m. and 3:00 p.m. My salary range is forty to fifty dollars per hour, negotiable." This target was so specific that we were able to find her the right role within a couple of weeks, and nine years later, she is still going strong there. This experience led me to create the *work-life triangle* as a way to help job seekers define their work relationship.

WORK-LIFE TRIANGLE

When it comes to work, getting the fit right is the most important thing for long-term satisfaction and success. And as a parent, your job-seeking time is limited. Once you know what you're looking for, you can tailor your job search accordingly and you can tell people more specifically what you're looking for so that they can help you.

If parenting has taught you anything, I hope it's that everything is a phase, nothing is permanent, and things can and will change.

The first thing you need to do is to define your own ideal work-life triangle. In a perfect world, where would you be working? What would you be doing? What would your schedule be like? How many hours per week would you be working? And what would be fair compensation for that work? Job seekers often believe there is a straight tradeoff between flexibility and compensation, but the reality is that the tradeoffs are much more nuanced for working parents.

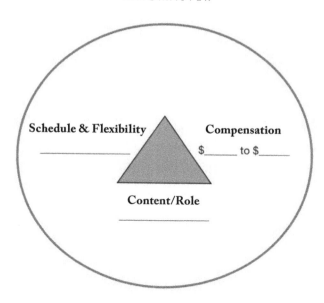

As you can see from the graphic, there isn't a straight tradeoff between schedule flexibility and dollars earned. Instead, the triangle has three sides: compensation, flexibility, and role. Take that dream-world scenario, when the stars align and you are working for an incredible boss, bringing home a respectable paycheck for doing work you love, and still being able to meet the bus in the afternoon. Put that into this graphic. That's right. Get out that pencil, and put it on the paper.

Next, circle the side of the triangle that's most important to you right now. Acknowledging that it will likely change, what is the most important priority in today's job search? That's where you will start your focus, and focusing will help you to evaluate the interdependencies of these factors. For many parents, it is flexibility. We will walk through some case studies of how different job-seeking parents have leveraged this model to start their searches.

But back here on Earth, we know the ideal situation rarely exists. And even if it did, like most things in life, it is subject to change. You could get that dream job with a ten-minute commute, but a new manager could take away your telecommuting day. Or the company could be sold. Or you might need to send your child to a new school across town.

If parenting has taught you anything, I hope it's that everything is a phase, nothing is permanent, and things can and will change. Best-laid plans and all. So instead of focusing *only* on the most ideal situation, you must determine acceptable ranges for each and acknowledge the interdependence of these factors. And there are infinite combinations!

ROLE

Let's start with the role. What is it you want to be doing? Is it what you are currently doing? A promotion? What you were doing before you left the workforce for caregiving? I know it sounds basic, but you need to answer this question: "What job do I want?" Depending on your compensation and flexibility requirements, you may need to adjust your target role. For example, if you were a project coordinator before maternity leave but compensation is a higher priority than the role, you probably need to look for more traditional project manager jobs. In chapter 2, we will focus on how to close this type of gap. List those target roles on your triangle.

FLEXIBILITY

There are more definitions of flexibility than there are Cheerios under the car seat in your minivan. It means something different to everyone. It may mean working from home one day per week, or it could be a 7:30 a.m. to 4:00 p.m. schedule. It may mean you just need to work from home occasionally around snow days or doctor's appointments. While few organizations have truly gone to a results-only work environment (ROWE), many have embraced flexibility as the standard. Think about what flexibility arrangements you need right now, including your must-haves and nice-to-haves, and jot down some notes on your triangle. One great resource for the various types of flexibility options many organizations offer is Werk.co.

COMPENSATION

Compensation seems pretty straightforward. You probably have some minimum number you need to make to meet your family's budget requirements. Have you done your research on fair compensation using tools like Glassdoor.com and Payscale.com? You will likely have a range here, particularly when you factor in benefits and look at the big picture of total compensation.

The mistake most people make when thinking about compensation is making the assumption that more flexibility in a particular role means less money. It shouldn't, by the way. If you're knocking it out of the park, why would it matter if you work from home on Tuesdays? But in some organizations it does, and more flexibility means you are on a lower-earning track. We have a long way to go on the stigma around flexibility. You can appreciate and be grateful for your flexibility, but don't apologize for it. This is a theme you will see repeated here often. The one exception here is that if you are working less than full time, you should reasonably expect a proportionate compensation decrease. That's just math.

You can appreciate and be grateful for your
flexibility, but don't apologize for it.

CASE STUDIES

Everyone's work-life triangle will look a little bit different. My own triangle has probably changed a half dozen times since I became a mom seventeen years ago! But seeing how others approached this exercise may help you evaluate your own interdependencies of compensation, role, and flexibility. Let's take a look to see how job seekers I have worked with in the past have used the work-life triangle.

Casey: Flexibility Priority

When I first met Casey, mother of two daughters, she was returning to work after a five-year hiatus from the land of the W-2, where she had last worked as a marketing manager. Casey was juggling a daycare pickup and a school bus drop and wanted—*needed*—to be able to walk out of the office every day at 4:00 p.m. She also needed to work close to home; her pickup requirements didn't allow for a long commute. Because of her priority on flexibility, Casey accepted a lower role as a marketing coordinator because she valued her schedule more than the role or the compensation.

On the surface, this looks like Casey traded dollars for flexibility. But really, Casey prioritized location (for a shorter commute) in a role with less responsibility because of caregiving logistics. By taking a step back in terms of role, Casey gave up late nights at the office so that she could spend that time with her girls instead. This isn't a failure or a misstep; Casey was intentional. She realized that this was just one phase over a long career arc, and it was the right move for her and her family at that time.

Andy: Compensation Priority

Andy came to me, soon after his divorce was final, for help in his job search. His single-income status meant that compensation was his biggest priority. More than the role he was performing or the flexibility in his schedule, Andy needed to provide for his family. His post-settlement agreement meant that Andy had several days a week with no caregiving responsibilities. On those days, he was able to pile up late-night hours and go on business trips while focusing on metrics to drive up his bonus. Andy targeted promotion-level roles with the highest earning potential, with the hope that after absolutely killing it for a year he might earn some of the flexibility he desired.

Parents sometimes feel bad about prioritizing compensation over flexibility. Modern society sends us a lot of mixed signals about what we "should" be doing in our careers and lives, and it is easy to feel working parent guilt. But remember: providing for your family is every bit as important as being at every strings recital. There is no shame in your working parent game.

LeToya: Role Priority

LeToya was a new mom who had recently relocated to an unfamiliar city. She was eager to find a new job but felt strongly that she would only leave her new son in daycare if she was absolutely passionate about the work she was doing. That made her role her main priority. LeToya focused her job search on nonprofits that were in line with her areas of passion and applied for a variety of roles at different levels with wildly different compensation before landing a position as a program manager. Although she was barely breaking even after paying for daycare, LeToya felt that this role had upward potential and that after proving herself for a year she would see her compensation increase during the annual salary review we negotiated for her when she took the role.

The Center for American Progress has conducted extensive research on this topic and has determined that a worker loses three to four times his or her annual salary for each year out of the workforce in lifetime earnings. Policy and industry-driven solutions are not happening fast enough and are not near-term solutions; you are going to have to figure this out on your own. I strongly encourage you to evaluate the opportunity cost of leaving the workforce for an extended period of time using their childcare calculator: https://interactives. americanprogress.org/childcarecosts/. This easy-to-use tool helps you evaluate the interdependencies of compensation and childcare, which can help inform your trade-offs on your own work-life triangle.

Putting the Work-Life Triangle Together

The interplay of compensation between role and flexibility is always at play, and I hear a lot of new parents say, "Well that's it—I'm just going to quit. After paying for daycare, I'm only making sixteen dollars a day." I get it; that was absolutely the case when I returned to work after having the twins. Our nanny's compensation was nearly three quarters of my take-home pay. Many days, it didn't feel worth it.

But what *was* worth it? Staying in the game, staying in the workforce. The statistics around the exorbitant cost of childcare in the United States are staggering. According to a study by the Center for American Progress, in all fifty states, the costs of having two children in a daycare center exceeds the median price of rent. But leaving the labor force to save money on caregiving has significant long-term financial impacts on families. We can find a solution that works for you.

As you will read in the coming chapters, you must be strategic in how you approach a hiatus from the workforce for caregiving. You need to be intentional as you approach your job search. This juggle, it's a marathon. For better and worse, you will be the Ringmaster of your circus for a very long time.

CHAPTER 2

FINDING YOUR DREAM JOB

Whether you are looking for a new job (more money, better flexibility, or increased responsibility) or returning to work after a hiatus caring for your family, a job search as a parent is a different beast. You have more parameters on your search but less free time to conduct it.

You have already done the hard work of defining the work relationship and now have a very strong sense of what you want to be doing. Now that you know what you're looking for, you can be strategic with the limited time you have. It is highly unlikely you will see a job posting online, apply for it, and receive and accept an offer for your dream job. Once in a blue moon, that's the case, but overwhelmingly, you will find your dream job by leveraging your network. I will show you how in three simple steps.

STEP 1: COMPLETE THE JOB SEARCH TEMPLATE

This is not the most glamorous tool or groundbreaking approach to a job search, but it is simple and easy to use, and it will keep you focused in the limited time you have to find your dream role. The goal here is to create a clear road map for determining your dream (and in reality, acceptable) roles and lining up your professional and personal networks accordingly. The process also identifies holes in your network, and closing those gaps is a part of the process.

You can download a soft copy at jenniferfolsom.net/resources.html; I will walk you through each of the sections so you can use any tool—heck, even pen and paper—to get this going.

HOW DOES THE JOB SEARCH TEMPLATE WORK?

This spreadsheet will help focus your job search by allowing you to set parameters based on your work-life triangle and identify target organizations to home in on desired roles. This process helps you use your professional and personal contacts to network yourself into your dream job.

TARGET ORGANIZATIONS

There are a lot of employers out there, so you need to set basic parameters on location, size, mission, and industry. What companies do you love? Whom have you always admired? You can start with the "best of" lists or companies that promote flexible policies, but what you see in practice doesn't always follow. You will likely yield better and more accurate results from your network. Know that woman at the bus stop in heels? Where does she work? Draw from your life experiences, interests, and passions to identify realistic potential employers.

JOB FAMILIES AND ROLES

This might seem obvious, but it is very important to be aware of the nuances of job families and titles so that you're seeking the appropriate job level (e.g.

project coordinator versus project manager). If you are looking to jump from the commercial sector to nonprofit or from one industry to another, do the titles and role types change?

PROFESSIONAL CONTACTS

This is where you list anyone you know in your target organizations or anyone with your desired role in other organizations. The idea is to leverage your existing contacts in a smart way and fill in the holes in your professional network. You can do this by attending industry-specific events, using LinkedIn's search function for a "six degrees of separation" connection, and generally improving your elevator pitch so that you know what to say when someone asks, "How can I help with your search?"

STEP 2: CREATE YOUR ELEVATOR PITCH

Now you have defined your work relationship and identified target roles and organizations. You have all of the elements for a strong *elevator pitch*. Your elevator pitch is essentially a two-to-three-sentence personal brand summary that says who you are, what you are looking for, where your specific expertise lies, and why you are right for the job. Let's look at a few examples of weak and strong elevator pitches.

Weak: I am an IT project manager looking for a full-time job with some flexibility.

Strong: I am a business process management guru with five years of federal agency IT management experience and a PMP certification. I am returning to work after an eighteen-month hiatus for child-rearing.

I led multiple projects like this for a large consulting firm at the Department of Transportation right before my hiatus and want to bring my skills and expertise to a similar role in a smaller consulting firm with fewer overhead responsibilities.

Weak: I am looking for a job closer to home. I don't care what it is; I just need to be home by 3:30 p.m.

Strong: I am a staff accountant with expertise in the nonprofit sector looking for a role in Greenville with an organization that values its people and allows flexibility around core business hours.

Weak: I am an HR generalist but am overworked and underpaid in my current job. I need a new one, and to get out of nonprofits!

Strong: I am an HR generalist with ten years of experience looking for a leadership role in a for-profit organization, and am specifically interested in solving a company's pay equity challenges.

When you work out your elevator pitch, write it down. Say it aloud a hundred times, while you're folding laundry or on your commute. It only gets better with practice.

STEP 3: REVAMP YOUR RESUME (OR START OVER FROM SCRATCH)

In today's connected world, it seems a bit old-school, but resumes are still very much a key element in modern job searches. We will cover resumes more extensively in chapter 3, "Returning to Work after a Long Hiatus," but here are a few elements you need to consider:

OLD OR NEW?

Your first decision is whether to start with your last professional resume or start from scratch with a new one. There are pros and cons to each approach, but either way, you're essentially creating a new document—and it has to be perfect. Make your resume easy for the reader or hiring manager to locate by saving the document as "Jane Smith resume." Saving it as "resume" or "Jane's resume Fall 2009" is going to get it lost. Yes, the reader or hiring manager could "save as" and apply a new name, but she likely has fifty or more resumes in her inbox, and you don't want to get stuck in the black hole!

FORMAT

I am still a fan of the chronological resume format, but there are some real benefits to a functional format. This format essentially calls out key skills and experiences in bullet points in the main body and lists employment dates in the bottom half. This format may work best if you've had a very long paid employment gap, if you're looking to switch job families or industries, or if you're looking to leverage volunteer or community experience in your job search.

CONTACT INFORMATION

This might be the most important part! Right at the top, list your mobile phone number (does anyone still have a landline?), your LinkedIn profile name for easy connection and review, and a professional email address. I have seen some doozies over the years, and your job search email should not be cutesy, a shared family email, or a spousal address—just your.name@ majorwebmailcarrier.com. Momzmilkisbezt@XYZ.com, I'm looking at you.

PROFESSIONAL PROFILE

Professional profile, career objective, summary—call it what you want, but put it at the top of your resume, right below your contact information: who you are, what you do, and what you want in two to three sentences or key bullet points; the "meat" of your elevator pitch. Employers are inundated with resumes, and a recruiter is going to spend approximately fourteen seconds reviewing yours, so make it stand out with a strong introduction.

RELEVANT INFORMATION

If you have been out of college for more than a decade, your resume could easily be three or more pages long. Remember—recruiters are not getting past the top half of the first page. The key here is to include only relevant information. List all of your employment dates and organizations, but call out only the most important information for the job to which you are applying. This means you'll have several versions of your resume, each one tailored a bit differently. Yes, it's a lot of work, but it's worth it.

DITCH THE CUTESY TITLES

Believe me, I know firsthand just how hard you have worked raising your children, running your household, and heading every darned committee the school handed you. But please do not put "domestic manager" or "household CEO" on your resume. Just don't.

ADDRESS THE GAP

We tackle this in significant detail in chapter 3, but what (besides the obvious) have you been doing while out of the paid workforce? Hopefully you have done something that is related to an eventual return to the land of the W-2 employee. If you are an attorney who has taken CE classes to maintain a bar license, list "continuing education" with course titles and dates. If you have community or volunteer experience relevant to your career goals, list those. For example, if you are a volunteer Red Cross fundraiser, list that just as you would a paid job (most recent work experience, key accomplishments, dates), because it is absolutely relevant to your desire to return to the major nonprofit development world. If you are in human resources and you are on the committee to select and interview the school's new headmaster, or if you are a CPA serving as the PTA treasurer (bless your heart, thank you) with a $25,000 budget, list it!

REVIEW

Let me say it again: review, review, review. Ask your spouse to read it. Ask three friends to read it. Ask your former assistant who's now working as a manager to read it. Copy edit. Review for tone and intent. Your resume should have a minimum of five red-line edits before it goes in your outbox. Make sure it's relevant to current market conditions and most recent industry trends, and that it's typo-free. Typos are opportunity killers.

Set aside some quiet, uninterrupted hours to work on this. The resume, whether you are revising or rewriting, is a lengthy process. It is *hard* to condense decades of accomplishments to one or two pages!

But the process of doing it will prepare you for networking meetups and eventual interviews. You need to own your own story and be able to explain it confidently, as well as describe how your unique expertise solves an organization's problems. You will likely get your next job from someone you know, but the resume is a necessary evil in the job search process, your paper equivalent of an introduction, and it has to be perfect.

STEP 4: HIT THE BRICKS!

Once your job search template is complete, turn your focus to networking strategy. Do you have multiple contacts at one of your target organizations? That's a good place to start. Do you want to be a development coordinator at an association but don't know anyone in the nonprofit world? You probably need to build out your network there.

But you, Ringmaster, are very, *very* busy and do not have time for hours of weeknight networking events when you are supposed to be driving the hockey carpool. Instead, armed with your elevator pitch, start with your strongest advocates. Create your "job search team:" those cheerleaders, friends, former colleagues, and maybe even your former assistant. Reach out to these folks first. Share your resume, ask for honest feedback, and incorporate it. Tell them what you are looking for in your job search. Over and over, I am amazed at how invested cheerleaders are in the job search and how willing folks are to help. Take them up on it.

Now that you have warmed up your networking skills, armed with your resurrected resume, begin to rebuild your professional network to work your way into these roles. Ask everyone you know in your job search team if they know anyone with a job family role from your target list. Who on your PTA committee knows someone at the companies on your target list? One of the biggest advantages of job searching as a parent is that you now have this wide network of people in your lives—coaches and classroom parents and neighbors—who can help bolster your professional network.

But what happens if you don't know anyone at your top target organizations? Add the organizations on your target list to the "search" function on LinkedIn to find out who in your network's network (think six degrees of separation) works, or has worked, at that organization. Use the online introductions to get into those companies. While you're there, "follow" those companies on all social media platforms (particularly LinkedIn, Glassdoor, and Twitter) to look at internal job postings, recent hires, and press releases.

LINKEDIN AND THE MAGIC OF THE COFFEE CATCH-UP

I hesitate to spend so much time on a social network that will likely change, but for the last decade, LinkedIn has been the predominant professional networking social media platform. While some people refer to it as "Facebook for your career," that oversimplifies LinkedIn's impact and misses out on its primary value: The six degrees of separation. It's like Kevin Bacon is your career counselor! And unlike many of my young colleagues, you are probably old enough to get this reference.

While nothing beats your offline, in-real-life network, the most efficient way to develop your online network is LinkedIn. In fact, it may be the most important way actually to rally your network in real life.

First, I recommend you use LinkedIn for the following tasks:

- Build out your professional profile based on your resurrected resume. Use the online template to get recommendations from prior colleagues and managers. Remember the job descriptions you reviewed for the job families on your target list? Make sure the keywords from those job descriptions are on your LinkedIn profile, because that's how recruiters for those specific jobs are going to find you.

- Reconnect with *everyone* you've ever worked with. LinkedIn practically does this for you by matching up employment dates to other members with the same organizations and dates of employment; all you have to do is link up. Remember the bad old days when switching internet service providers meant switching email accounts? It was very easy to lose track of former colleagues, but LinkedIn makes it easy. With a wide employment gap, you're much more likely to be hired by someone you know, who knows your work and results, than you are by dropping an application into the black hole of a career site.

- Join industry- and job family-related groups. These are free and a great way for you to network with peers online. Learn about industry-specific job fairs and new policy and regulations in your field—and learn about job openings from group members. There's a fee for employers to post a job opening on LinkedIn, but it is free for group members within the group setting (under discussions), so many post there. One open secret is that if you are in the same group as another LinkedIn member, you can contact him or her directly, even if you aren't "linked" already. It's a great place for industry-specific networking.

You can use all sorts of online resources to rekindle your professional network and even expand it further, but it is the offline portion that is going to get you your next role. Nothing beats the face-to-face interaction and follow-up of an in-person meeting to build an actual relationship. And that's what the network is all about.

You can use all sorts of online resources to rekindle your professional network and even expand it further, but it is the offline portion that is going to get you your next role.

COFFEE

I am a big fan of "Hey, can I take you to coffee?" as the opening salvo to building a professional relationship. Twenty minutes, five bucks, and everybody loves the opportunity to talk about themselves over a mocha-whatever. If you have been following this process step by step, you are now networking yourself into your target roles and organizations, you have connected online, and you are now meeting in person. Do the research on your coffee date via LinkedIn, find out about the company and industry via other various resources, and ask very specific questions when you're together. Pick up the tab, send a thank-you email that day, and send a written thank-you note that night. In an online world, meeting in person and sending paper by snail mail sets you apart in a very crowded hiring market.

FOLLOW UP

Follow-up is a major key to rebuilding the professional network and the step most job-seekers overlook. Whether you're meeting someone at a networking event or over coffee, send an email right away and a written thank-you in the mail no later than the next day. If you are not already connected, send a LinkedIn connect request a few days later. I cannot overstate this. When busy people take time out of their day to help you, express sincere gratitude. Hopefully, in your relationship-building meeting, you learned something about the other person and can "pay it forward" with a favor or introduction for the other person; this is what we call good networking karma. If your coffee date is late because there was a plumbing emergency at home, email over a great recommendation from the plumber you've used. If he or she mentions really struggling with a business problem, forward an article you've recently read on the topic.

AVOIDING THE RESUME BLACK HOLE

The only black hole bigger than your sock-eating clothes dryer is the resume inbox. I am here to tell you is that 99.9 percent of the time, you will not get a job by applying blindly online. It's just not going to happen. In any market, but particularly in a market where you're one of hundreds applying for a single role, you must have someone on the inside to physically walk your resume over to the hiring manager's desk and follow up to gain valuable feedback.

How do you get someone on the inside, you ask? Thanks to the job search template approach, you are likely applying for roles where you have some connection, a contact, or a contact's contact. But if you truly cannot find a person "IRL," as the teenagers say, exploit LinkedIn's most valuable function: search.

To leverage the "people search" function, enter the organization to which you would like to apply. Anyone in your immediate network work there now or in the past? Perfect—link up to that person if you haven't already, and let him or her know you're applying. Ask for help in the process. Ingratiate yourself. Buy the person lunch or coffee, and send a thank-you email immediately and then a written thank-you note. It's a crowded market; you need to stand out.

No one in your immediate network related to that organization? No problem. That's where the beauty of LinkedIn really shines. You have access to your network's network, like a giant game of six degrees of separation. Identify secondary or even tertiary contacts, and select "get introduced." This allows your common contact to make an easy online introduction, and you two can link up.

Once linked, ask your new inside contact a couple of questions about the position. Thank the person profusely for his or her time, and if the new contact offers more help, take him or her up on it. Again, buy lunch or coffee, and again, send a thank-you email immediately and a written thank-you note straight away. And thank your contact who made the introduction. Gratitude is free and is your secret weapon to getting the job you want. The timing of the gratitude is key. An immediate email demonstrates enthusiasm, and a written thank-you note several days later keeps you on the person's radar.

THE BOTTOM LINE

There is no secret sauce here. You need to put yourself out there, do the relationship work, and follow up. While online resources can expand your network and even show you connections you didn't know existed, you cannot hide behind your laptop. Pick up the phone. Make a coffee date. Send a thank-you note. That's how you get your dream job.

CHAPTER 3

RETURNING TO WORK AFTER A LONG HIATUS

Despite all of your best work-life strategies, perhaps you have been forced into taking a long hiatus from working outside the home. Or, even better, you made the conscious decision to spend time away from your career to focus on caregiving. Either way, parents who return to work after a long hiatus face an uphill battle. According to the Center for American Progress, workers can expect to forego three to four times their annual salary over the course of their careers for each year out of the workforce. With the rapid rise of technology, skills can become obsolete within three years. This is overwhelming, I know. What you need to remember is that although the market may not respect your decision to stay home with your children, you must own that decision and hit the challenges head-on.

Although the market may not respect your decision to stay home with your children, you must own that decision and hit the challenges head-on.

Returning to work after a long hiatus requires a souped-up version of the job search strategy from chapter 2. Each of the elements is even more important and requires even more time and preparation. But alas, you don't have childcare while you are not working and can only relegate so many screen hours to *PAW Patrol*. You must use your time wisely, be efficient, and attack this job search with confidence and a road map.

USE YOUR DIGITAL TOOLS

If you have three children two to three years apart and waited until the youngest went to school to return to work, LinkedIn didn't exist when you last pulled a W-2. Without an online presence, you practically don't exist. In fact, unless a candidate is a referral, I likely won't interview a candidate without a strong online presence.

Why? Because it's your first introduction, your instant first credibility check. I am selfish with my own most precious resource—time—and won't conduct an interview, sales call, or networking meeting if I can't "see" this person online first. Keep this in mind when building out your online profiles, particularly on LinkedIn.

Take care to ensure that the resume you've updated, the one with the killer professional summary and community and volunteer "employment" dates in the job history section, is uploaded in your profile. Many online algorithms won't pick up candidates in recruiting searches if there is an arbitrary length of time from last employment. No, you don't forget everything you know about accounting while getting through the pureed foods and sleep-training stages; that is simply the way recruiters cull candidates.

ADDRESS THE GAP

It bears repeating: the market will not respect your decision to leave the workplace. Your future employer is concerned about things like, "Are her skills stale? Can she keep up with rapidly changing technology? Will she fit in here? Can she pull the extra hours when needed?" I know that the years out of the workforce have brought you all sorts of new skills, like time management and conflict resolution, and have rebuilt your character in terms of resilience and patience, but your future employer does not care about that.

Don't be mad about that; your future employer has one objective: hire the best person possible to solve an organizational problem. You must enter this job search with the knowledge that you have the professional skills to do the job *and* a growing toolkit of soft skills from parenthood that are actually a rock-star combination. Let that sink in to give you the confidence to overcome this uphill battle.

In the meantime, you need to assuage the fears of your potential future employer head-on. In chapter 6, "Your Off-Ramping Plan," we will go into greater detail on what to do while out of the workforce to make your eventual return go more smoothly. Here is a sample of the concerns a potential employer may have about a candidate who's been out of the game for a while:

> **Concern:** Stale professional skills
> **Solution:** Keep current or update your professional certifications through continuing education credits. A current nursing license or project management professional (PMP) certification says, "I'm ready to hit the ground running tomorrow."

> **Concern:** Not up to speed on technology
> **Solution:** Demonstrate in your resume, on your LinkedIn profile, and in interview talking points how you leverage current technological solutions in your volunteer work. For example, how you moved all of the church's working documents to Google Docs in your role as recording secretary for the lay leadership

committee. Or how you set up a Slack channel for the crew parents' association to improve communicate during regattas.

Concern: Out of touch with industry trends
Solution: To demonstrate to potential employers that you are staying current, share topical articles on LinkedIn or other social media outlets, or in email as you are rebuilding your professional network, to show your interest in and knowledge of what's happening in your industry. If there has been a major move in your industry, say from programming in SAS to programming in open source solutions like R, take an online course and get a certification. This demonstrates that you understand that the market has changed since you last lived in a cube farm, and you have taken steps to reconcile this. Not only that, but you have independently verified your skills, which goes a lot further than simply listing a skill on your resume.

HAVE YOUR STORY DOWN

The elevator pitch is important in any job search, but is vital for parents who are returning to work. You have done the hard work of defining your work-life triangle and putting together your job search strategy, and you know your elevator pitch. This is your three-sentence personal branding spiel that tells everyone you know who you are and what you want to be doing. But you need to address that gap in your resume.

The biggest issues I see with the elevator pitch in parents returning to work all stem from a lack of confidence or preparation. When addressing the gap, I often hear women using vocal tics like "uptalking" (ending a declarative sentence with higher intonation, indicating a question), vocal fry (low, gravelly tone), or speaking in trailing, run-on sentences.

Look, you've done the hard work to prepare for this job search; own the gap. You know the market may not respect your decision (even if it wasn't much of a choice) to stay home, but by golly, you know it was worth it. You are smarter, stronger, and more valuable because of that experience. So with your head held high, a soft but focused gaze, and just the slightest smile, practice that elevator pitch. Be concise, be confident, and move on.

Here are some examples of what not to say and, more importantly, what *to* say in your elevator pitch when addressing your employment gap. None of this is spin; it's all true. The reasons you left your last job, decided to stay home with your children, or are going back to work now are your reasons alone. For these purposes, think about what your future employer wants to hear.

> **What not to say:** "I've been a SAHM [stay-at-home mom] for the last twelve years, but now I'm going back to work because my kids are almost out of the house, and well, college …"
>
> **Instead, try this:** "After some time at home for caregiving, I am eager to return to my professional passion as a physical therapist. My license was renewed last year, and I've been volunteering in the high school training room the last two years."

> **What not to say:** "I was a marketing manager at a major national bank for ten years, but for the last five, I've been the CEO of Willingham Family, Incorporated, because the bank was so inflexible to my parenting needs."
>
> **Instead, try this:** "I took an intentional pause from my career in financial services marketing leadership

and am looking to bring my expertise to a similar role with a regional bank. Over the last five years, I've pursued a series of digital and content marketing certifications through the Hubspot Academy to learn how to bring the latest marketing techniques to a staid industry."

What not to say: "I was a teacher before I had kids, but once my second child was born, I quit because daycare for two exceeded my salary. I'm going back to work now because my oldest is in school."

Instead, try this: "I am looking for a role in a nonprofit association that leverages my teaching expertise. Over the last year, I took several online courses with MOOCs [massive online open classrooms] and am eager to combine my classroom and online learning experience with a nonprofit that focuses on children."

PREPARE YOURSELF

You have heard this safety briefing a thousand times: "In an emergency, put your oxygen mask on before helping others, including your children." This is a very hard concept to put into practice as a mother, but it is extremely important when returning to work after a long hiatus. In fact, one of the most frustrating groups of candidates I have ever worked with is moms returning to work.

Why? Because you are so used to putting yourself last that you don't know how to prioritize yourself. Call it the martyr complex, imposter syndrome, or maybe just guilt about not pulling down a paycheck the past few years, but women who have been out of the workforce for long enough resist spending money on anything related to a job search.

It's time to invest in yourself. Spend the money on a review course, an online certification, or a resume-building workshop. Get a real, honest-to-God, grown-up haircut (not the walk-in place where you take your six year old). Get a new suit or interview separates, an outfit that fits your current body and makes you feel like a million bucks. Putting yourself back out there is scary, and you need all of the confidence boosters you can make.

PREPARE YOUR FAMILY

This often overlooked topic can easily threaten the success of a parent's return to work. If your family is used to you doing everything—from packing lunches to delivering forgotten violins to school—they will have a rude awakening when you're working for someone else. Take Sara, a dear friend of mine and mom of three who stayed at home for fifteen years raising her family and taking on every community volunteer role possible. Sara went to nursing school and eventually went back to work in a hospital but hadn't negotiated a few predictable challenges with her husband. When he missed the inevitable sick kid call (his first ever!) from the elementary school clinic because she was in a lab, things came to a head.

This is one of the most overlooked steps in returning to work after a long hiatus: preparing your family. While you may have been "encouraged" by your spouse to stop volunteering so damned much and actually get paid for the work you're doing, or your kids may be cheerleading you with *"Go, Mom!"* when you head out the door in a power suit for your interview, the truth is that not being at your family's beck and call will be a shock to the family dynamic.

And you can't wait until you are actually working to have these discussions. The outcome may inform your search. For example, if your spouse has frequent travel, you may have to lean more on the flexibility side of your work-life triangle in crafting your job search. But you need to hash it out now, not when you are a week into your new gig and your husband is on the jetway boarding a flight to Duluth, and you get the inevitable "Your son had an accident on the playground at recess." Life will throw you curveballs; you can't always save the day.

Life will throw you curveballs; you can't always save the day.

THE BIG TALK

It is time for the big talk with your significant other. If you have been running the home for the last few years, those responsibilities have to be divided and conquered. We go into greater detail on this in chapter 9, "Sharing the Load," but while you are interviewing, you need to accept that things will not be the same as they have been and start working it out. Take my advice, nearly two decades into the working mom adventure: play to your partner's strengths. My husband is an expert laundry folder, and in a household with three boys, I do two loads every day and leave the folding to him after bedtime. And praise substantially! If this method doesn't work, make a list of everything that needs to be done on a daily basis and find a fair and equitable way to divide household responsibilities. And remember—something's got to give. One look at my lawn and flower beds full of weeds shows what "gave" in our house this year.

I suggest you hash out the following topics before you even interview for the first time:

- Who will do pick-up and drop-off?

- How do you decide who stays home for a snow day? Sick child?

- Who will you call if you get stuck in traffic and can't meet the bus?

- Who are your backup calls for before and after school? Are those contacts in both parents' phones?

THE BIG TALK, PART 2

It's time for the kids to get straight on what's happening. If you've been staying home with them, they're likely used to a built-in playmate, driver-to-friends, picker-upper of all toys, and last-minute classroom cupcake manager. Be frank with them, hand over age-appropriate tasks where strengths and interests lie, and let go of ideals of perfection. I cringe every time I see the bulging, cramped drawers of my sons' dressers, but they put their own clothes away, which is one less task on my to-do list. But let me warn you: there will come a time when your son forgot his diorama and "Mom, could you just bring it to school?", and you'll have to say, "No, tiger, I am on my second day of work; this one is on you." I am terrible at this. I still feel guilty. I still occasionally tear up about it. But (theoretically, anyway) it builds responsibility, grit, and accountability—all traits we want to see in our children.

CHILDCARE

It seems like a chicken-and-egg scenario, but you need your childcare set up in advance of having a job. If you apply for a job to our company, I expect you to be available to interview on one business day's notice. That is just the way it is. We are all working at the employer's convenience. And if we present you with an opportunity and you say that you need a month's notice to start because you don't have childcare lined up, we likely won't bring you another opportunity. It's time to call in favors from friends, family, and neighbors. Put them on notice. Pay favors forward for backup babysitting so you can call them in when needed. One of the best strategies I've seen from our candidate on the childcare front was a woman who—listening to my advice to invest in herself—booked a sitter for two mornings a week. She used these six hours to interview a full-time caregiver for her eventual return to work, job hunt aggressively, and set up informational interviews. When I called her for interview availability, she simply said, "Sure! Any time between 9:00 a.m. and 1:00 p.m., Tuesday or Thursday."

We've covered your job search if you have had a hiatus for caregiving. But what if you already have a job (or two, technically, since you are a working parent) and need to find a new one? That's your job search on steroids. Read on.

CHAPTER 4

CHANGING JOBS

If your job is not working for you and your family, it's time for a new gig. Ringmaster, it's time to shine the spotlight on your work ring. But a job search is its own full-time job, and as a parent with a job, you already have two of those! Job searching while parenting leverages the same framework from chapter 2, but on steroids. You don't have a minute to waste. Changing jobs as a working parent requires a highly targeted, highly efficient strategy that wastes no time.

GET YOUR HOUSE IN ORDER

I don't know about you, but whenever I am embarking on a major transition—whether it's a much-deserved vacation or relocating to a new residence—I have to get my house in order. Out with the old. Getting really clear on what I am doing and how I want to do it. And how I want things to look at the end, whether that's walking back in from vacation or living in a new home. The analogy holds true with a job search while parenting: out with the old, get organized, and move efficiently to where you want to be.

JOB TARGET CLARITY

In the first two chapters, you spent considerable time defining your work relationship triangle, determining your acceptable boundaries for schedule flexibility, compensation, and role. In chapter 2, you focused on target organizations, the roles you were going after, and your network connections to get you there. In chapter 3, you focused on rebuilding your network and addressing a resume gap if this job search was your first after a hiatus for caregiving. Now we will talk about the three most common job searches for parents who are currently working: more flexibility, higher compensation, or a "bigger," promotion-oriented role.

That previously-equilateral "define the work relationship" triangle (DTWR) has shifted, and one of the sides is now more important. As we have discussed, your situation, needs, and desires change over time. The triangle shifts and angles become a little more obtuse or acute (my teenagers will correct my geometry on this one), but the framework and process hold.

MORE FLEXIBILITY

If you don't have the flexibility you want and need, I strongly recommend that you try to negotiate this first in your current role (see breakout box). Particularly in the case of parents returning to the same role after maternity leave, I find the work expectation is that you can and will be able to work like you worked before. Before you produced a new life. Before you fed the baby every three hours (even overnight!) and still came back to work after a short ten-week leave. Before your world was turned upside down. Whether these expectations are self-imposed or you're feeling the side-eye when you slink out at 5:15 p.m. to make a daycare pickup, work changes after you have a baby. It just does. It has to.

If you are unable to negotiate the flexibility you desire in your current role, it may be time for a new job. For example, maybe you have a new boss who believes in 100 percent face time in the office and you would like a new one who understands that two year-olds sometimes get ear infections in the middle of the night and you can't predict when you will need to work from home or go to the pediatrician. Or maybe your five year-old is graduating from daycare and heading to kindergarten (hallelujah!), and you want to shift your hours to be there at 4:15 p.m. to meet the bus. No matter the reason, get really clear on what's not working and what you want.

Flexibility is the most nebulous factor on which to evaluate new opportunities. Your needs change over time, policies are enforced inconsistently, and it means something different to everyone. Your clarity, specifically knowing exactly what you need to make things work, will help.

So rather than focusing on companies with a certain policy (e.g. companies with stated policies that allow telecommuting one day per week after six months of service, pending manager approval), it is likely more effective to search for a new organization with a more family-friendly or flexible culture. Rather than examining company policies, instead focus your search on managers who value results over face time.

When developing your target list of organizations, you looked to your "lists" (e.g. top ten best places for working mothers), but also your own life, such as who was in heels and lipstick at the bus stop. If flexibility is your main job search driver, take this a step further. Ask everyone you know in your industry about their flexibility accommodations, managers, and organizational culture. Have that elevator pitch ready:

"I love my job, but I just can't travel like I used to. My goal is to get it to about 20 percent, not 50 percent. You're in consulting; how much are you on the road?"

"I don't think the partner life is for me, and I'm looking to go in-house. Do you know anyone in the general counsel's office at work? What are their hours like? Would you be willing to connect me with someone there?"

"I see you at soccer practice at 5:00 p.m. twice a week. How did you swing that? Does your firm hire IT project managers? Because that's the type of flexibility I'm looking for, flexing around core business hours."

We will go deeper into this notion in chapter 5, "Rocking the Job You Have," but flexibility and your overall job satisfaction are almost always driven more by your manager than your organization. It's your boss who determines when you can leave the office every day and whether you are entitled to a full bonus even though you shifted down to an 85 percent schedule.

As you are networking, make it clear that you are looking for a great boss. In your job search template, highlight and prioritize the contacts that you think would make great bosses. Don't get hung up on the fact that this guy used to work for you ten years ago; sometimes that happens. He was on the fast track while you were having three kids. You both won.

Reach out to contacts who know you, your work ethic, and the quality of your work product. They won't need to stand over your shoulder to make sure proposals are created to their liking and get submitted on time. *Micromanagement kills schedule flexibility.* To combat it, you need a boss who trusts you.

Micromanagement kills schedule flexibility. To combat it, you need a boss who trusts you.

BIGGER ROLE

Maybe you have been on a self-imposed career plateau while keeping small people alive, or perhaps you have been placed on the "mommy track." Or maybe you want to kick your career up a notch. Whatever you want, don't feel guilty about wanting it; ambitious working moms are a beautiful thing! No matter the reason, it's time for a bigger role. One with more responsibility. A role with more prestige. It probably comes with more money, but also with longer hours and travel.

This job search will have fewer targets. The goal is to identify the two or three jobs where you are the only candidate they want to hire. Remember—you are being hired to solve a business problem, not "do a job." You want to be the best of the best, the one candidate whose unique experience will save the day and knock their socks off. While this requires a lot more up-front research, networking, and analysis, it will pay off in the end. Because even though you are ramping up your career and will have more demands on your work life, you are still a parent. You likely still need more than twelve hours' notice to travel. There will be snow days. You will want to take vacations around school holidays.

The big takeaway here is to make them fall in love with you before hitting them with the big flexibility ask. When the role is what's most important, the job search and interview process is not the time to discuss flexibility. Instead, be so uniquely qualified to solve that organization's problems that you get hired for that big role. Then, as we learn in chapter 5, "Rocking the Job You Have," you will be in a great position to negotiate for—or, hell, just take—the flexibility you need.

MORE MONEY

One of the most frustrating realities in the American workplace is that in order to make substantially more money, you need to switch jobs. Typical annual salary rises of 1–4 percent mean that the new guy or gal coming in at your level (or even below you) will make more than you in about three years. Even if you get promoted, there is a strong likelihood that your new compensation is on the lower rung of the salary band. So if you have been chugging along, doing a great job and working with a boss and schedule that work for you, you will eventually be frustrated enough or motivated enough to seek greater compensation elsewhere.

As a manager, I try to combat this by making sure my rock stars are on the promotion path, and I lobby hard to get them off of the bottom of the salary range. I know my best talent will be lured elsewhere. But corporate policies and traditions for salary adjustments are formidable opponents.

In an era focused on gender pay equity (but still with so much farther to go!), there is a tremendous amount of transparency in compensation. Use this to your advantage. Glassdoor.com has surprisingly accurate self-reported salary levels, and LinkedIn predicts compensation for each role posted. What does a senior financial analyst make in larger firms? Smaller boutique firms? If you are reviewing open roles posted on LinkedIn, how does your experience compare to the requirements? How do your current and target compensation compare?

The "more money" job search tracks closely with the "bigger role" search. Even though a similar role at another organization may net a bigger paycheck, you need to position yourself as seeking a bigger career opportunity to solve that organization's problems. No one wants to hire someone who's only in it for the bigger paycheck. Target organizations that value what you bring to the table, and the money will follow.

Target organizations that value what you bring to the table, and the money will follow.

Don't overlook benefits when it comes to evaluating total compensation. Even though you typically don't get detailed information on the value of benefits until further into the interview process, it is a mistake to consider salary alone. Does an organization offer free health care to employees? Student loan repayments? Backup daycare subsidies? Free parking or a Metro subsidy? Glassdoor.com's benefits summaries and reviews can yield good intelligence here. These benefits can often add up to five digits and should not be overlooked.

RESUME

Over the last two decades of reviewing resumes, I can say it is more art than science and largely a stylistic endeavor. Ask a dozen experts on the do's and don'ts of resumes, and you will likely get a dozen different perspectives. But most of us agree the format must be consistent with industry standards, it must contain only relevant information for the job to which you are applying, and it must be error-free.

But as I read through mountains of resumes every day, I'm struck by how many seemingly little things can derail an otherwise fantastic resume. Here are a few tips from the resume *reader's* perspective:

- Put the **meat up top, in bold.** Have a security clearance? PMP? CPA? Put that up front, on top, in bold. Most readers won't get through the second half of your resume, where many job search candidates like to hide training and certification information. A recruiter spends an average of fourteen seconds on your resume; you need to grab that person's attention up front.

- As we saw in chapter 2 (Step 3), you need to save your **resume document name** as "Jane Smith resume," to keep your resume out of the black hole. A simple and straightforward name makes it easy for hiring managers to keep track of you.

- Get a **professional email address**. Go to Gmail and get a free email address that says something like "Jane.Smith@gmail. com." They'll give you options if yours is taken, but please don't conduct job search correspondence from mommyjane@ something.com or anything related to family, kids, sports, or hobbies. First and last name, that's it.

- In chapter 2, we went into great detail on the tactical steps for avoiding the resume black hole. Don't miss any of these steps.

SOCIAL MEDIA AND OVERALL ONLINE PRESENCE

Now that your resume is in good shape, make sure your LinkedIn does the following:

- Reflects your most current role and accomplishments

- Has a current, professional photo of you

- Is set to let recruiters know you're open (under "Career Interests"; this is blocked from users at your firm)

- Includes a written recommendation from a recognized LinkedIn user

- Reflects not only the job you have (under "Skills and Endorsements"), but also the job you want

Likewise, it is time to make sure your overall social media presence is in good shape. Anything involving heavy booze, politics, or sensitive topics has to go. Your recruiter and future manager will Google you, search your public information on Facebook, and research what others have to say about you on LinkedIn. Google yourself and see what comes up. Untag yourself from the picture of you doing the beer bong at your little sister's bachelorette party and delete the angry tweet about the last election. It's just not worth it.

TOP TEN LIST FOR OUTREACH

Going back to your job search template, with extreme clarity on your job search goals, who in your network are your top ten targets? Who is in a position to hire you today? Who can refer you to a hiring manager for a job that is currently open? Who gives the best feedback and advice? Rank your top ten contacts in order. Next, send an email with your elevator pitch, attached resume, and an explanation of why you want to meet with them. Provide three dates and times for a coffee date at a location convenient to them. Pick up the tab (keep the receipt—I'm no CPA, but I hear it's a job search expense for itemized deductions!), and send a thank-you email note that day and a follow-up written thank-you in the mail.

WHAT TO DO IF YOUR JOB SEARCH DRAGS ON

Job searches can be physically, emotionally, and mentally exhausting. You are already living the two-shift life as a working parent and are adding a major initiative to your crowded day. Even with the most efficient, strategic job search, it can sometimes drag on. And that, understandably, can feel a little defeating. If this happens to you, don't do these three things:

DON'T GET DISCOURAGED

Job searches can take months. Even while you're doing everything right, there are elements of luck and timing that are simply beyond your control. Consider the time of year you are searching. No hiring occurs in December and August. It's a weird factor of scheduling and decision-making around hiring managers' vacations. It's a tough time to start a job search, and if you are in this time period, you should just bake that into your schedule. Likewise, certain industries have busy months where—despite a "hot" opening—organizations can't get it together to put a smooth recruiting process together. You know your industry, so keep that in mind. Stay positive, and if you need to take a break to get your head in the right space, take it.

DON'T KEEP DOING THE SAME THING

If what you are doing isn't working, it's time to switch up your approach. Take a deep breath, and figure out where you are getting hung up.

Are you getting zero nibbles after sending out dozens of resumes? Revisit your job search template contacts. Do you have enough of the right contacts? It probably makes sense to work on building up your networks in those areas. Try industry-based networking events through your professional association or even social meetup (like meetup.com) groups.

Is your resume dying after one touch? Reach out to five new contacts inside and outside of your industry. Ask for feedback—people love to be asked their opinion—but also ask for red-line edits. There may be something unintentionally off-putting, such as an error earlier editors missed, or you may just not be telling the right story about your career and how that translates to what you want to be doing next.

Getting the interview but not the offer? Reconsider how much time you put into preparing for the interview. Did you tap into all of your resources, online and in real life? Put your big girl pants on and call the hiring manager for some feedback. Inhale, exhale, and accept that feedback. This isn't a character flaw; it's about getting better at interviewing so that you can get that job you want.

DON'T GET DESPERATE

There's a reason recruiting and dating have so many trite analogies. In efficient markets, both parties are looking for a love match. Remember that desperate guy that kept asking you out in college, no matter how many different ways you said no? Ick. Don't be that guy. Hiring managers can smell desperation, and it is the most unappealing characteristic in a candidate.

Why? Because as a hiring manager, I want to invest in a new employee that's going to be passionate about the work. One who jumps out of bed in the morning with a dozen new ideas on how to get the job done better and faster. I want to hire someone who lives and breathes this stuff, who really *wants* this job. I don't want to hire someone who is just looking for the next job, any job. Because I know that I will spend the time and money to bring that candidate on board and he or she will be gone the second a better-fitting role appears.

Even if for all the right reasons, you need the next job, any job, to pay the rent or to get out of a toxic work environment, resist the urge to get desperate. Stick to your strategy; you are better and stronger than you know. You are enough. And if you keep at it, the right role will come along.

THE INTERVIEW

Okay, Ringmaster. You have done the hard work of getting that interview. Don't blow it with a lack of preparation! Interviews are never easy, and the skill comes more naturally to some than to others. But that's just what it is, a skill, and it must be practiced. If you've been out of the workforce for more than five years, it's perfectly conceivable you haven't interviewed in the better part of a decade. You need to prepare, practice, and follow up.

PREPARE

Know everything you can about the company and the organization. Use LinkedIn to find an "insider" in your network's network who can give you the inside scoop.

- **Industry:** Review industry and trade publications, and set up a Google alert for daily or weekly updates for what is going on in your industry. Join industry groups on LinkedIn, and attend an in-person session or webinar from one of those events. You want to have stories, statistics, and facts about your industry at your fingertips while interviewing. If you are lacking industry preparation, you appear aloof and disinterested in the role to which you are applying.

- **Company:** Aside from website research, follow the company on LinkedIn, Twitter, and Facebook to get a sense of the culture, trends, and most recent news releases. Review the company interview section on Glassdoor.com. Past interviewees often post interview questions and their candidate experience feedback.

- **People:** Review the LinkedIn profiles of the managers with whom you'll be interviewing. Follow them on Twitter and search on YouTube for any speaking engagement videos. Do you have any people in common? That's the fastest way to warm up an interviewer. Any common interests that you can divine from social media? Hit those early. You want to make a connection as quickly as possible with the interviewer to keep the interview going and to drive a next step in the hiring process.

From there, develop a thoughtful list of questions that demonstrate your industry and company knowledge. You want to appear both knowledgeable and curious. You are informed, but not a know-it-all. You have a sincere interest in the role and are passionate about the industry.

PRACTICE

It sounds silly, but you need to do some mock interviews. Ask your spouse, neighbor, or best friend to grill you. Start out with easy, standard interview questions, such as "Walk me through your resume," "Tell me about your strengths and weaknesses," and "Tell me about a time when ...." Then try and get to more difficult questions. You want these answers to be polished and roll off your tongue. The most difficult question to answer is "How can you transition back to work after such a long employment gap?" (or some variation thereof). Have this answer ready. It might be something like "I've been a member of XYZ industry group, attended networking events, learned about recent policy changes, such as ABC law, and have volunteered on such-and-such committee." If you're a bookkeeper, let the interviewer know that you took an online course to get certified in the latest QuickBooks version. Demonstrate enthusiastically that you're prepared to hit the ground running with minimal on-ramp time.

You need to be able to synthesize your resume—a summary of your entire career—into a succinct story that explains to the interviewer why you and your unique experiences alone are a perfect fit for this job. A combination of stories (e.g. "When my boss went on maternity leave as we were facing a negative cash-flow quarter, I needed to step up to find ways to improve profitability") and hard facts (e.g. "I reduced overhead expenses by 22 percent by reevaluating all vendors") will leave a positive, lasting impression that you are the best candidate for this job.

FOLLOW UP

Similar to the networking informational interview, this is the part that most jobseekers forget. Ask for a business card from each person with whom you interview. Send a thank-you email immediately and a written thank-you (on professional cardstock) straight away. Be specific in your interest and sincere in your gratitude.

NOT GETTING THE JOB

An abundance of research, as well as my anecdotal experience, shows that women typically apply or put themselves up for a job or promotion only when they feel they are close to 100 percent qualified for the role. Not surprisingly, men do the same with about 60 percent confidence. This lack of confidence, coupled with fear of not getting the job, keeps women from tossing their hats into the ring for jobs for which they are eminently capable and qualified.

Recently I have had close friends and colleagues experience the crushing disappointment of not getting a job they wanted. In a number of cases, they were jobs the candidate didn't seek out, or even particularly want, but the confidence blow of not being the one to say no took significant tolls. For several of these women, it took them out of the job search game due to the risk of feeling unwanted, of feeling like professional crap.

That's nonsense. If you didn't get the job, it wasn't the right one for you. Call the hiring manager and ask for feedback, and you will likely hear that another candidate had more of one kind of experience or another that you don't have. You can't create that experience out of thin air. If it's important to you, go out and get it. If it's not, look for similar roles that don't value that experience as much.

At the end of the day, it's not personal. Someone else was the better fit. Maybe they were cheaper or more experienced in a particular target market. Despite transparent and widely accessible tools, finding the "right fit" next job is an incredibly inefficient and exhausting process. Keep your head up, and march on.

CHAPTER 5

ROCKING THE JOB YOU HAVE

It started like any other day. The alarm went off at 4:40 a.m., I went for a quick run, and then I came back to prep that evening's dinner. My husband, a bike commuter, was up and out by 6:00 a.m. I served two seatings of hot breakfast and hustled the twins to their bus stop by 7:30, and my then-second grader to his by 8:30. Somewhere in there, I showered and dressed for work, all the while answering emails on voice-to-text about that morning's big pitch, which I had been preparing all week, and blow-drying my hair for some semblance of a professional appearance.

Yes, it was chaotic, but I was getting it all done. I'd hit my stride. I hopped in the car with my next-door neighbor, an AMLAW 100 Big Law firm partner, to carpool downtown to work. Buoyed by confidence, I smiled and chatted with my neighbor while sitting in traffic on the 14th Street Bridge, content that at that exact moment, this supermom had it all. It was then that I got a call from my youngest son's principal.

The principal—a dear friend and perfectly reasonable man—informed me that my youngest son had to be picked up immediately for fighting on the school bus or else risk referral to in-school suspension, which would end up on the dreaded "permanent record." What should I do? Pick him up and miss the major pitch scheduled for 9:30? Leave him there in ISS, thereby ensuring a life of crime?

With tears stinging my eyes and working-mom guilt settling in quickly, I hopped out of the car and into traffic on Constitution Avenue. I hailed a cab to turn back south toward home and our neighborhood school to pick up my little delinquent, all the while cursing myself for thinking I "had it all figured out."

If you are awesome at your job, you can command the flexibility you need.

But there was the pitch. To a new, *huge* client, one that was going to be all mine. If I closed this deal, I would hit my revenue goal for the year. How was it possible that I could be hurtling back toward home instead of putting work first? The only reason I could take off at the last minute was because I had rocked this job hard for the last three years. I had built a solid team that could step in for me at a moment's notice. I had built such significant social capital with my peers and colleagues that when I called in a favor, they knew it was for real. So after three years of over-delivering and producing stellar results with no drama, when I called my boss to tell him he'd have to do the pitch without me, his reply was this: "Take care of what you need to, I'll let you know how it goes."

The big idea here—and one that is missing from most conversations about working parenthood—is that as a parent, it's more important than ever to rock your job because you *will* need flexibility. Daycare *will* call to let you know that your child is running a 102-degree fever. The end-of-school-year party *will* be at 2:00 p.m. on a weekday. Your kid *will* get in a fight on the bus and make you miss an important pitch. In short, if you are *awesome* at your job, you can command the flexibility you need.

Most of what you've read about work-life balance or integration is from the employee's perspective. "How to Get a Flexible Job," "How to Work as a Part-Time Partner Track Lawyer," "How to Negotiate a Flexible Schedule." But in real life, your boss will make decisions concerning your flexibility, not you. And so you will have much greater success if you approach this tightrope walk from the employer's perspective.

The dirty little secret that no one wants to talk about is this: if you are awesome at your job, you can command all of the flexibility you want and need. You heard that right: be the absolute best whatever-it-is-you-do, and your company will bend over backward to make accommodations for you.

I know, I know, you're thinking, "But what about the six-month probationary period before working from home?" and "What will people think if I leave at 4:30 p.m. every day?", and the bottom line is this: it doesn't matter. Kick ass in your job every day, make your boss's life easier, be polite and friendly with everyone, and you can leave the office when you need to leave.

If you are absolutely the best communications and marketing manager this nonprofit has ever had and you have a nanny crisis on your fourth day on the job and need to leave, are you going to get fired? No. Of course not. If you are rocking the job from day one, approaching challenges with a good attitude (and this is key!), and focusing on results, you will be just fine. Let's dig a little deeper on this.

ROCK THE JOB FROM DAY ONE

There are lots of books on this topic. I am a big fan of Michael Watkin's 'The First 90 Days, and I strongly encourage you to add this to your reading list. Gather all your job search and interview process data and convert it to your action plan. Seriously, as soon as you sign that offer of employment, take that job search spreadsheet and put that into a one-to-two-page document summarizing the following:

- What you learned about the organization while doing your research (historic challenges, big opportunities, market or industry data)

- What you learned during the interview process (new boss's wishes, team attitudes, biggest organizational hurdle in the next six months)

- Your goals for yourself in this new role (e.g. revamping the weekly internal newsletter and raising the open rate to 65 percent)

Whether you're coming back to work after a hiatus or have taken a new role for a different reason, you will probably feel a little wobbly at first. This is normal. This shows that you know the stakes are high. And that's okay. As a working parent, your stress level is higher than those without little people at home, and your time is limited.

Refer back to this document to remind yourself why you are there and what you came to do. Put your energy and time there, and let the rest go. Again, I'm going to harp on the idea that a good attitude matters. If you are stressed out or anxious or pissed off, you need to check that at the door. What I am *not* advocating for is a sunny, happy disposition 100 percent of the time; I get it, things go south. You were up all night with a vomiting child, and your new coworker dumped a half-done project on your desk this morning, but if you are pleasant, calm, and direct, you will be able to keep it all together. We will talk about strategies for stress management in chapter 13, "Managing the Stress," but it's worth a reminder here.

FOCUS ON THESE THREE THINGS (AND LET THE REST GO)

No matter your new job, you need to focus on three things:

1. Doing the job you were hired to do

2. Making your boss's life and work easier

3. Communicating results

DO THE JOB YOU WERE HIRED TO DO

This sounds obvious, but start with the position description. After you have been on-boarded, if your organization doesn't have a formal goal-setting process, schedule a goal-setting session with your new boss. Review the position description and convert those responsibilities to fifteen-, thirty-, sixty-, and ninety-day goals. Include a section for who is responsible for training you on various topics or getting you up to speed, and determine a metric for measuring success. After that, figure out how to get a quick fifteen-minute "huddle" (it's not meeting, because your new boss is too busy for meetings, right?) at least every two weeks (but preferably more regularly) to check in on progress.

Some organizations will have this "set goals and establish regular progress checks" carpet laid out for you, but most will not. When there is an open position, members of an organization are doing their jobs *plus* a portion of someone else's. They are overwhelmed and are thankful that a competent person is there to share the burden. If you show up with a thoughtful, coherent plan for transition, it will go a long way toward showing that you are competent and confident, intend to contribute meaningfully, and are worthy of independent work.

So if you show up and there's no transition-in plan, start here. What you want is clarity and certainty on your responsibilities, as well as direction on the training and briefings you need to get there. You also need clarity on how you report status, resource needs, and completion of tasks. The table below is a good and simple way to get started.

Task	Person Responsible for Training	Date	Metric
Update corporate blog	Jenny Smith, External Communications	31 January	Error-free postings, 300 hits per week
Employee handbook updates	Katie Smithson, Human Resources	15 February	Meet all draft and publications deadlines

Overwhelmingly, I see new hires fail because they think they were hired to do the job as it was written on the position description. It's true, but doesn't go far enough. New hire, I'm talking to you: *you were hired to solve a problem.* Figure out what that problem is and how to solve it. It might spill out of the role you were hired for. In fact, it probably will. Meeting that challenge is what you were *actually* hired for.

The near-term goal here is to build a solid, trust-based relationship with your boss from day one. You must understand the context of your job, the *real* problem you were hired to solve, and how you can communicate progress toward solving that problem on an ongoing basis.

MAKE YOUR BOSS'S LIFE EASIER

This isn't about sucking up to your new boss. Being a suck-up is the fastest way to alienate your new colleagues, and you need them almost as much as you need your new boss. This is about getting on your side the person who controls your destiny, your compensation, your promotion track, and what time you leave the office every day. And that's a smart move. As a working parent, you will need more flexibility to manage your life outside of the office, and you need a solid, trusting relationship with your boss to make that happen. So, how do you do that?

DISCUSS COMMUNICATION STYLES

This may sound pedantic, but ask direct questions about how your boss likes to communicate. Nothing is more irritating than when a new hire interrupts an important call with a time-sensitive but low-importance question. You might try:

- "If I have a time-sensitive question, how do you want me to ask you? Is it better to interrupt a meeting, or should I use Slack [or whichever IM your organization uses]?"

- "Is it better for me to cover my progress every week in an ad hoc huddle, a weekly standing meeting, or a regular email update so that you know what I am working on?"

- "Is it helpful for you to know my weekly objectives on Monday morning? Do you want a follow up on Friday as well? I can let you know what progress I have made and where I'm running into roadblocks."

REVIEW CALENDAR, ANTICIPATE NEEDS

One of the most valuable things my top lieutenant does for me is to review my calendar several times per week and help me prepare for events and meetings *before I even ask her.* She will notice conflicts where meetings out of the office are scheduled too closely together, prepare research or talking points, and connect things I am working on to what she sees in other parts of the organization. I have never—*not once*—said no to any schedule or flexibility request; she provides value tenfold to her stated role.

- If your organization does not make individual calendars public, ask your boss if you can have access to hers. If there are privacy concerns, she can make individual appointments private, limiting access. I don't need to know when she is going to the dentist. But in a trust-based relationship, your boss will not only see but appreciate the value of having someone else in her corner to prepare for the week ahead. If public or shared calendars aren't culturally acceptable in your organization, cover important upcoming events in your regular check-in meetings. By being proactive instead of reactive, you are helping to reduce her stress level and improve her own performance.

- Review upcoming meetings, and offer to help. My marketing coordinator will often send me an email that says, "Hey, I saw a meeting about the APDU conference on Thursday. Is it that time of year already? Would it be helpful if I attended and brought last year's materials for us to review?" Um, yes please, thank you very much.

- Appeal to her human side. Your boss is a human. She has a life too, and like it or not, that affects work. My colleague leaves me samples of the fresh-ground peanut butter from Whole Foods that I can't have in our house (kids and their darned peanut allergies!) on my desk when she sees my stress level is sky-high. When I lost my best friend after a three-year battle with pancreatic cancer, my team did everything they could to isolate me from any BS work in the office and didn't take it personally when my mood was very, very low.

COMPASS CHECK

We all have the professional dream where we sail in at the last minute to save the day with a perfectly-crafted deliverable the boss did not even know he needed. That doesn't work in real life. I love seeing my team members head-down, fully engaged in a big piece of work, but going full steam in the wrong direction will leave both boss and employee extremely frustrated. It's not a sign of weakness to want to know if your work is what is being asked of you. This is particularly true if you do not have a bird's-eye view of the whole problem or process, or if this is a new deliverable or work product. Try doing this instead:

- "I think I understand what you are looking for in this memo; would it be okay if I popped by in two hours with an outline to see if I have the audience level and content we discussed adequately covered?"

- "I am not sure I know enough about this topic to cover it in a slide deck to the whole firm. How about I send you what I have by the end of the day and we can pull in other resources if I don't have the full picture?"

- "Before I go whole hog on this brief, is it okay if I shoot you a template with dummy language to see if that hits the mark on what we're trying to convey?"

COMMUNICATE RESULTS

You laid strong groundwork with your biweekly check-ins with your new boss. The next step is one that is often forgotten, leading to a post-honeymoon job slump: ongoing communication with your boss. I know that this sounds boring and mundane, and if you are a professional, you might think you've got this covered. But trust me, at the end of your ninety-day transition, you need to set the stage for how your boss wants to communicate with you.

By establishing when you are going to communicate, you will not need the random check-ins that could kill a flexible work environment. A boss that is constantly trying to track you down for answers to questions will balk at expanding—or even keeping—a flexible or remote work situation. Once that trust is broken, it is very difficult to repair.

If there is a problem, speak up early. Bad news does not get better with age.

Start the conversation with something like this:

> "Thank you for so much hands-on support while I learn the ropes of this job. I know your time is valuable. I want to communicate how things are going in the way that works best for you. Would you prefer a weekly check-in meeting? Daily email summaries?"

I know you're thinking this is overkill, but I cannot repeat this enough: the key to combating micromanagement (the death knell of flexible work arrangements) is building trust and communicating results. You will not have any flexibility or the elusive work-life balance if you are answering emails from your boss at 10:28 p.m. about small details on a project due tomorrow. Communicate positive results early and often so that your boss knows the job is not only being done, but being done *well*, even if your butt is not in a seat at 6:00 p.m. If there is a problem, speak up early. Bad news does not get better with age. You want to avoid the perception that the problem occurred because you were working from home or because you left at 4:00 p.m. to get to soccer pickup. In fact, you want to demonstrate your ability to solve problems no matter when they occur or where you are working. If trust is not established early, it is next to impossible to rebuild or repair. Get the relationship with your boss right, and the rest will fall into place.

WHY DO FLEXIBLE WORK ARRANGEMENTS SOMETIMES FAIL?

When flexible arrangements fail, it is most often because of a lack of trust and a breakdown of communication. A leader who is not sure what her staff is doing every day and is nervous that something will fall through the cracks will micromanage because it's *her* arse that is on the line. The antidote to this dilemma is to start from day one by building trust with your leader, communicating results early and often, and overdelivering. If you feel like that trust is wavering or that there is tension in your relationship, put on your big girl panties and ask a direct question about what might be wrong.

Here are some ways to start that conversation:

- "I have noticed that you are having an especially busy week. Is there something I could be doing more or differently to help?"

- "Is it still okay that I leave at 4:00 p.m. today? I know you have had back-to-back meetings today just after returning from vacation. Would you like for me to make arrangements to stay later and give you a hand? I'm more than happy to."

- "I know I have had a million questions lately, I don't want to annoy you with constant pop-ins while you're preparing for the big brief. Would instant message work better, or is there someone else familiar with this process who could help?"

BUILDING STRATEGIC RELATIONSHIPS (AND FORGETTING THE REST)

A working parent's most precious resource is time. When it comes to building relationships in your new job or within your industry, you cannot afford to waste even one hour. It may sound shallow, but you need to be highly strategic with the relationships you build internally and externally to your organization. Up front, you need to identify who is important and how to connect.

INTERNAL (WITHIN YOUR ORGANIZATION)

First of all, you must be unfailingly pleasant and polite to everyone. It is not as hard as it sounds. There is no time in your day for drama or difficult relationships. This is so basic it hurts, but do it: greet every coworker with a smile and make direct eye contact, minimal chit-chat required.

Early on, identify who in the organization matters to getting your job done. Your boss? That is easy. You have got that covered. Think long and hard about where hang-ups in your day might happen. Is it a counterpart in another business unit? Mary in Accounting who drafts your invoices? The administrative assistant who controls the conference rooms? Find those people, figure out what makes them tick, and proactively make their lives easier. This positive workplace karma will pay you back tenfold.

Not everyone needs to like you, nor should they. You are an adult, and this is a job, not high school. Be polite, be respectful, and let the rest of it go.

Also, people need to know who *you* are, and fast. Volunteer for a committee that has high visibility— say, corporate philanthropy, which plans one big event per year that the C-level executives attend. Do not volunteer for any social or "sunshine" committees; to quote Elaine Benes from *Seinfeld*, in an office setting, every day is "someone's special day." You'll be on Safeway bakery cake pickup duty on a weekly basis (probably feeling guilty you didn't bake something yourself, as ridiculous as that sounds). Pick something you enjoy, preferably something that happens once or twice per year and that has wide recognition. People need to know who you are, but you do not have time to run an internal ad campaign.

Better yet? Write a summary of the event in a short article for your intranet or internal newsletter. Suddenly, everyone will associate your name with that event or committee, even if they haven't seen your face yet.

Want to know what you don't have time for? Being popular. Not everyone needs to like you, nor should they. You are an adult, and this is a job, not high school. Be polite, be respectful, and let the rest of it go.

I remember when I first went back to work after the twins were born. They were six months old, I was starting a new job at a Big Four consulting firm immediately after 9/11. It was an intense time in Washington, D.C., and I was making a career pivot from finance into management consulting just as the financial markets fell apart.

I negotiated a flexible, early schedule (7:00 a.m. to 4:00 p.m., plus post-bedtime email check-in with the West Coast team), and frankly, the job was not that hard. You want to know what *was* hard? Worrying all the time about what people thought of me. Stressing out about my reputation, not wanting to be disliked by my colleagues for sneaking out the door at 4:00 p.m. to relieve the nanny. Paying said nanny time-and-a-half so I could attend every single happy hour for birthdays and promotions and engagements. Interpreting every terse email as a slight or thinking every time I was interrupted in a meeting that my colleague (or boss or client) did not think I was capable of doing my job.

I wasted emotional energy and social capital trying to be well-liked. I wasn't strategic as to with whom I built relationships. Looking back, those were the biggest mistakes in my first role as a working parent. You do not have to attend every single happy hour, just the ones that really matter. And how do you know which ones matter? Any major milestones for your boss, your assistant, or your second-in-command.

EXTERNAL (OUTSIDE YOUR ORGANIZATION)

If you do not think you have time for networking and relationship-building *inside* your organization, then you *really* don't have time for it *outside* your job. But you need to, and here is why. According to the Bureau of Labor Statistics, the average American stays in his or her job for 4.2 years. This means if your organization's promotion cycle is two to three years, you will likely get promoted only once by your boss before wanting or needing a new job. You *just* spent untold hours and energy getting this job; do you really want to start from scratch again in four years? This should light a fire under you to understand the importance of building and maintaining a network *outside* of your organization.

Seriously, do the math. You will need that motivator to get to the networking event after you have rushed home, put dinner on the table, started your seventh grader on math homework, and wrangled a toddler. It reminds me of the time I did the math on how much each class cost me in undergrad. Once I realized that every single Survey of English Literature 8:30 a.m. class with Professor Dal Wooten was worth $238, I never skipped again.

But again, I know your time is your most valuable resource. How can you make both family time and networking happen? By being very strategic.

INDIVIDUAL NETWORKING

Think about the individuals in your life and work that matter most to you, the ones you *don't* work with right now. Find a way to stay connected with them, and by golly, **schedule it.** I know this is about as romantic as scheduling sex with your spouse, but putting it on the calendar is the only way to get this done.

Who falls in this category? Maybe your last boss before you took maternity leave. Perhaps it is a favorite graduate school professor (hello, Ken Homa!) or your former assistant who is now three levels higher; it really does not matter. Professional relationships that really click are rare, and they take effort and commitment to keep up. Put a quarterly reminder on your calendar to reach out to these folks, and aim for every other connection to be in person.

I'm a big fan of the coffee date. It's thirty to forty-five minutes, costs ten dollars, and can be squeezed into a packed calendar. Come prepared to discuss one big topic or something you would like the other person's advice on, but focus on what your work mate needs. Ask lots of questions. Offer to help or make referrals, and for heaven's sake, follow up.

GROUP NETWORKING

Ahh, the group networking event. Here in Washington, D.C., you could attend three of these a night if you wanted to, full of a diet of bad white wine spritzers and mini-quiches. On the one hand, they are an efficient way to meet or keep up with a lot of people. On the other, the relationships are often superficial, and this is pure torture for introverts.

The way to make these groups work for you is to be strategic and to go deep. If you hold a professional certification, particularly one that requires continuing education credit, join that organization, go to events, get your credits, and mingle. Knock all of that out in one to two events per year. If you are a CPA, you probably want to join your local AICPA chapter. If you have any human resources certificates, you know that SHRM (Society of Human Resources Management) is not only a strong national organization but also has local networking events that provide much-needed continuing education classes to maintain your credentials.

But the secret sauce is getting really involved and seeking prominent or leadership roles in one of these organizations. Rather than being a surface-level player in four or five organizations, find one that helps grow your network and where you feel the most comfortable, and really go deep.

What does "going deep" mean? It means raising your hand, volunteering, leading, being "out there." Like dating, you may have to kiss a number of proverbial frogs before you find your people. But when you do, it won't feel like extra work. My secret tip is to get on the membership committee. It is high visibility to organizational leaders, and you get to meet all new and potential members before they even walk in the door.

HOW DO YOU FIND THE RIGHT GROUP?

In a word, *ask!* And be okay with the fact that your group may need to change over time.

As an entrepreneur, I was a founding member, group leader, and big cheerleader of Her Corner, an organization that supports the growth of female-led companies. These were my *people,* y'all. I lived for their events. But once I made the tough decision to put my own business on the shelf when my largest client created a spot on their management team for me, I felt lost. When women there asked what I did for a living, I felt a bit like a fraud attending a networking group for female entrepreneurs when I had—at least for the time being—become a corporate hack. While I still cheer loudly for these women, I knew I had to find a new professional group but did not know where.

By asking those individuals with whom I networked on a quarterly basis, I was able to come up with two strong organizations that feel right for where I am professionally and are in the Venn diagram sweet spot of being comfortable enough for me to make a priority but still push me out of my comfort zone.

ONE STEP FURTHER: THOUGHT LEADERSHIP

Okay Wonder Woman, you are rocking your new job, you are getting coffee on a regular basis with a few key influencers, and you are on a committee in a professional organization that feels right for you. What do you do in your (ha!) free time? Time to amplify your brand and let that thought leadership flow!

Now, I know you consider it a success if you show up to the office without a yet-to-be-determined schmutz stain on your jacket and manage to send two network-related emails per month. I do, too. But I am here to tell you that being a thought leader can be done. Once again, by being strategic and planning well, you can minimize your time and maximize your exposure to let the beautiful, freaky supernova that you are shine through to the entire world.

CREATE SHAREABLE CONTENT

If you are looking to take your thought leadership showcase up a notch, consider a blog. Or infographic. Or podcast. Write and create content that highlights the brilliant musings dancing across your brain (typically at 2:00 a.m.). Writing on a regular basis covering topics about which you are passionate and that relate to your work will not only hone your writing skills, but will also demonstrate that you are a leader in your field. It will show that you care about these topics, you research them on your own time, and you make an effort to share helpful content with your colleagues.

This is someone a hiring manager will want to bring on board. This is someone a manager wants to promote. This is someone teaming partners and community organizations are seeking out. Further, if you are looking to negotiate some sort of flexibility into your schedule, you need to be a rock star. It's as simple as that. If you want a new job that lets you leave to meet the school bus three days per week while still making solid compensation in a field you love, you need to demonstrate that you are worth it.

SO I WROTE A FEW BLOG POSTS; WHAT DO I DO WITH THEM?

At the time of publishing, Medium is the go-to platform for composing and publishing blog posts outside of your own organization's website. With its strong interoperability to other platforms, content is more likely to go viral. But down the road, I know there will be other platforms; don't let that hold you up. Start writing and sharing, and here are a few ways to share:

- **Submit to an industry association.** Associations are always looking for guest authors and new (free!) content for their print and written magazines. Who knows? If the piece gains traction, you could be asked to be on a panel at a networking lunch or to speak at a conference, the holy grail of demonstrating thought leadership.

- **Share on LinkedIn.** The "old way" was to post a link to your blog post in your LinkedIn status bar, but LinkedIn's new Publisher tool will help land your content as a news item in your contacts' news feed. Powerful. You can draft your blog post wherever and copy and paste it into the Publisher window.

- **Share a link with contacts.** Need an excuse to connect with a former colleague or the industry bigwig you met at a conference last year? Send a link to your blog with a brief, customized email that says, "I wrote this, and I thought of you because …"

- **Add recent blog posts to your email signature block if your corporate style guide allows it.** Readers will see that you are writing regularly and may even click through to your link.

SOCIAL MEDIA FOR PROFESSIONALS

I believe in good social media karma. If you are a positive member of your industry's social media community, good things will come back to you threefold. Share news items that are relevant to your industry colleagues, whether or not you wrote them. Congratulate someone on a new position.

Attending a conference? The conference hashtag is your new best friend. The conference likely has a social media manager who is following the hashtag and will retweet your comments. Take photos, highlight a speaker's main points, and you will be seen as someone to follow. Remember—the further along you are in your career, the more the market demands thought leadership. This is an efficient way to showcase it.

FALLING OFF THE TIGHTROPE: WHEN LIFE HAPPENS

Life happens to, well, all of us. Just when you think you have it all figured out, your elderly mother falls and needs hip replacement surgery. Or your husband has a bike accident. Or your son breaks his arm on the playground at school.

If you have rocked your job since the day you walked in the door, you have built social capital with your colleagues and trust with your boss. If you have been the best whatever-you-do in your field this organization has ever seen, they will likely bend over backward to accommodate your needs. When you fall off the tightrope that is working parenthood, take these steps so that when the tragedy *du jour* has been resolved, you are able to climb right back onto the rope:

1. **Address the issue directly and promptly.** When life happens, call your boss (or better yet, meet in person) and explain what happened (with only as much detail as is relevant to your job), any flexibility accommodations you may need, and how it impacts others in the organization.

2. **Present the solution.** If you are going to be out of the office, invariably, your work will not get done. Or it will fall to someone else. Make a plan for how you can keep the trains moving while you are not around. Present it as a plan to your boss, not as an ask. When possible, present options, such as "Would you prefer that I come in abbreviated hours daily or continue working full-time but from home during this time?" Presenting options lets your boss have some control over an otherwise uncontrollable situation.

3. **Say thank you.** To everyone. To the boss that supports your flexible work arrangement. To the coworkers that pick up the slack while you are out of the office. Put it in writing. Express

appreciation, and then move on. Everyone has life events; it was just your turn.

4. **Pay it back.** Just as "scorekeeping" doesn't work in marriages, keeping tally marks on who is covering for whom does not work well in the office. But if you are continuously paying it forward, picking up the slack for others, and filling in gaps where needed, that social capital will be available to you when you need it. And you *will* need it.

CHAPTER 6

YOUR OFF-RAMPING PLAN

Ever hear the term *work wife?* It's your partner when you're at the office, your better half, the one you can't work without. My "work wife" was with me for three consecutive jobs but, at the conclusion of a large project, decided to stay at home for two years until her youngest went to kindergarten. With ten years of management consulting experience and an MBA from a top-rated school, she knew she would eventually want to return to the corporate world. Right then and there, we mapped out a plan for her inevitable return on a cocktail napkin. We envisioned what her resume should look like in two years and developed a strategy for how to make that future resume a reality while serving as chief water bottle filler for her two sons. And sure enough, by following our plan, she positioned herself to ensure a smooth reentry to the full-time workforce.

Work wife is hardly alone. Whether by choice or circumstance, many women will take time out of the paid workforce for caregiving. The 15 percent of (previously working) moms of newborns who don't immediately return to work likely will at some point. And as detailed in chapter 3, "Returning to Work after a Long Hiatus," if you do none of the things in this plan, I can guarantee you a rough, uphill battle.

But it doesn't have to be this way!

In this chapter, I will help you plan the transition from a full-time job to off-ramping for a stay at home and out of the paid workforce for one to five years. This plan will help you minimize the financial impact and future job search pain.

IMAGINE YOUR FUTURE SELF

The most important step is this: imagine your future self. As a seasoned parent (ha!), you know enough to know that all sorts of things change, that nothing is constant in your circus. And while it is tempting to yell, "Peace out!" on your last day in the office without a plan other than preschool playground lunches, you need to think about how long you will be out and what you want to be doing upon your return. For example, if you are having your second child and want to stay at home until your oldest goes to kindergarten, your plan can be, say, returning to work in a contract role in digital marketing around "school bus hours" in the fall of 2023.

And you need to imagine what the *future you* wants to say in an interview during the summer of 2023. What activities will you have for the dates your resume says you were out of the workforce? How will you answer questions about what you have been doing while away from the workforce? How will you allay fears that you are out of touch? That your skills are dated? That your ramp-up time will be too long? Let's take these one at a time.

> **Concern:** Skills and capabilities are dated
> **Solution:** Take an online course. "Mommy brain" is a real thing. Trust me. I've had it. While Junior is napping, you can take a course on a MOOC (massive online open classroom like Coursera) to keep your mind sharp and skills up to date, and prove to the world with a grade and actual certificate that you

still bring your A game to the show. Anything that is verifiable, such as an industry-wide recognizable brand or certification, goes a long way toward proving your skills. You're not just saying you have bookkeeping skills; you have the Quickbooks "certified user" badge to prove it.

Concern: Out of touch with industry trends

Solution: Join your professional association *and* attend local networking events. Keep those CE (continuing education) credits comin'! You will keep your professional certifications active, stay on top of current industry trends, and build your network in a highly targeted way. That guy you chatted with over coffee and Danish at the SHRM (Society of Human Resources Management) local chapter event? He could be your boss in two years. Take it a step further and join the association's LinkedIn group. Set up Google alerts for key trends. Read those articles, post them on LinkedIn to show that you are staying up to speed with your field, and proactively share interesting articles with contacts in that space. This becomes an easy habit when you sit down with your laptop during nap time. Step away from Pinterest, and when that Google email comes in with the digest of timely industry articles, share away!

Concern: Long ramp-up time

Solution: If your industry and role allow for this, consider freelancing, even for a very small project. If you helped edit a friend's business plan or designed a new school logo, these projects can be listed on your resume under "Freelance Whatever" for the time period you are out of the workforce. You prove that your skills are sharp, that you are using the latest technology, like Google Docs and Slack channels, and that you will hit the ground running if hired.

Concern: Limited network
Solution: Volunteer strategically. Here's a hint: Not at your kid's preschool. You'll be there anyway. But if you want to return to a position in nonprofit fundraising, don't chair the annual silent auction committee; join the local Red Cross chapter and run their annual campaign. That position can serve as a "job" on your resume to address the employment gap, keeps your skills fresh, and most importantly, expands your network beyond the playground.

A note about the costs of these things. Yes, most of these actions come with an associated price tag, namely in babysitting for your little people while you do some of these things. Stay-at-home parents can be challenging candidates to work with for their refusal to invest in (read: spend money on) themselves. Ringmaster, you are in control, and you are worth the cost of an online course or travel to an industry conference. If you are getting grief from your spouse about spending money now to keep your skills up to date, remind him or her that you will eventually be going back to work and that this minimizes the financial impact in the long run.

MINIMIZING THE FINANCIAL IMPACT

As we learned in chapter 3, time out of the paid workforce—even a short amount of time—can have a tremendous impact on your lifetime earnings. According to the Center for American Progress, a working mother can expect to lose three to four times annual earnings for every year out of the workforce. This is a monster of an impact over earnings lifetime. In fact, CAP created an online childcare cost calculator for parents to calculate the explicit and hidden costs of leaving the workforce to become a full-time caregiver. Try it; it's eye-opening. Even after doing the math, leaving the workforce still may be the right choice for you and your family, but having a solid off-ramping plan will minimize the long-term financial impact of this decision.

The on-ramp back to work doesn't have to be hard if you're prepared for it.

CHAPTER 7

BLURRED LINES: THE REALITY OF THE NEW HOME OFFICE

Once solely the domain of privileged knowledge workers, mainly women, telecommuting has become the norm across most industries and many job types. Originally a hard-to-get benefit for only the most trusted and revered talent, thanks to technology and increased pressure on profit margins, you're seeing everyone from hourly call center workers to nurses delivering telemedicine from the sanctity of their homes. Some people work from home occasionally, such as with a sick child, and others will work remotely as a permanent solution.

While this setup has obvious and pretty significant benefits, it can also squash all hopes of a work-life boundary. The home office is the ultimate "blurred line."

Working from home will only be successful if you set ground rules. Taking an 8:00 a.m. video conference while trying to get your toddler dressed and your eight year-old to the bus stop? Talk about a clown show! Whether you're part of the growing freelance economy or flexing your schedule to work around school bus hours, you need to find a way to work at home. You may be lucky enough to have a separate space with a door, or you may prop your laptop on the kitchen island among lunchboxes and chemistry notebooks; either way, you'll need to develop a strategy for being productive at home.

ESTABLISHING A WORK SPACE

Most remote workers will tell you that it's best if you can find a separate space that is specific to your work. This is particularly true if you spend a lot of time on the phone or on video. Nothing chips away at your credibility like a dog barking or kid babbling in the background of a big call you're leading. If your children are young and are at home with a babysitter (and you need a sitter; if you are working from home, you need to be actually working and not caregiving—that's not negotiable), then a door is a helpful signal that you are working and should only be interrupted for blood or fire.

But most of us don't have the luxury of an entire home office, and it's helpful to designate a corner that is just for your work space. Several of the successful telecommuters I spoke with said they designated a corner of the master bedroom for this, as it is already a "no touch" grown-up space with specific access rules for young children. I have never been a good sleeper, so this doesn't work for me; I can't have my laptop staring at me from across the room while doing my evening sleep stories on the Calm app. This is a highly personal decision; you need to figure out how work works for you.

And even if you create the perfect setup, this is another area that may change as your kids get older. When my children were younger, I shared a home office with my husband. Because we rarely worked from home on the same day, this worked. I spent a lot of time on the phone and needed the quiet. That meant my older two shared a room, but so be it. This job paid the mortgage on that shared room!

But a few years ago, we renovated our house and eliminated the home office. We simply weren't using it. It was designed for an era of desktops and multiple giant monitors and huge printers and lots and lots of paper. With laptops and older children and the widespread use of Google Docs and DropBox, my home office is now just these things:

- Laptop

- Mobile document scanner

- Headset

- Filebox

I still keep a small, wireless printer on a file cabinet in our guest room. I can't give up on paper altogether, but the footprint of the modern remote worker is much smaller. As my kids got older, I found I could work among them in the afternoon, sitting shoulder to shoulder while I scheduled meetings and they worked on homework. If your children are young, take heed. They will soon be old enough to keep their sticky fingers off of your work things so that you can leave them on the kitchen island.

Here's the bottom line: You need an intentional space for remote work. It can't be random, and the others in your home need to recognize it.

SETTING BOUNDARIES

You are working, not surfing, so the large and small people with whom you live need to know when not to disturb you. My former boss, who worked from home every Friday, had a picture of his head on the body of a dragon on his home office door. When that picture is on the office door, dad is working. Interrupt dad for something short of an emergency and you get Dragon Dad. And nobody wants Dragon Dad.

STRUCTURING YOUR DAY

How you structure your day is intensely personal. Depending on your family and client needs, you need to do what works for you to minimize your distractions and maximize your productivity. Can't do conference calls at 7:30 a.m. because that's when you are trying to feed kids and get them out the door? Try and avoid them, while identifying that time of day when you are free to talk without distraction.

Elizabeth Duffy, mother of three and president of the Federal Affairs Office in Washington, D.C., has this advice:

> Don't start work wearing what you slept in—get dressed. Next, prioritize what has to get done during a regular work day versus what you can do after dinner or when the kids are in bed. Make sure you meet with clients, colleagues, someone, *anyone* at least twice per week. Smile and forgive those who think working from home is not really working—you're not going to change their minds.

Katy Kunkel, New Zealand transplant to McLean, Virginia, who leads global marketing and strategy projects while not mothering her four says this:

> Start with coffee and reading something to set the tone for the day. Check email and social media at regular intervals, no more than three times per day. Get a stand-up desk and switch up work area depending on your assignment. Leave the housework and dinner prep until when the kids are home; you won't be able to focus then anyway.

Here's the bottom line: the day won't go the way you want it if you let others control it. Find the time when you are most productive and most able to interact with others, and maneuver your schedule around that.

MAGIC TIME

I bet this is where you thought I would tell you that you must draw the line with your work, set boundaries, and log off. Wrong. I'm a boss, I have clients, and I live in the real world. Like it or not, the market expects more time than you can give. You need an extra five to ten hours of time per week to work, and it needs to be as seamless as possible to everyone. You know your boss is expecting an email response before the next business day as you rush out of the office at five-fifteen to get Sally to soccer. Play to your strengths and family schedule to squeeze that in. When my boys were younger and had a seven o'clock bedtime, I would log back in from seven-thirty to nine-thirty, rounding out the day with a West Coast team I supervised. Now that they're older, I set my alarm at the ungodly hour of 4:40 a.m. to in get a workout and one to two hours of work before the day starts. Pick one, but don't do both; that's a recipe for burnout.

VIRTUAL FACE TIME

If you're remote, you need to stay relevant and connected. Get comfortable with video. Pro tip: elevate your laptop on a book so that the camera is at eye level, and you'll eliminate the double chin that has you looking like your Aunt Lois on screen. Be on chat or instant messaging—present, but not attention-seeking. Find fun and creative ways to stay connected, like with a "flashback Friday" playlist that you compile from recommendations and share. I kick off my week by asking my team, including remote staff, a "Monday share" question about the weekend or a getting-to-know-you-better question like "What superpower would you want?" Mine? Being in two places at once: home and work.

While many professionals will only work from home occasionally, such as on snow days or one day per pay period, others will make it the standard of their workday solution. On the extreme end, we find freelancers, those lone wolves who comprise the gig economy. The 1099 world is a different beast from your standard W-2 employee situation, so let's dig deeper into the complexities of this arrangement.

FREELANCING

With the growth of the gig economy—comprising nearly a quarter of Americans in 2016, and disproportionately working mothers, according to a study by the National Association of Counties—there is a good chance that you will at some point pursue freelance work. To better understand how to make this work, I sat down with Kim Gallagher, mother of four with twenty years of experience as a successful freelance creative director and copywriter. Here is Kim's advice on making freelancing work for you:

PORTFOLIO DIVERSITY

Treat your client work like an investment portfolio: diversity is king. You need diversity of industry (e.g. healthcare is a constant, while technology can be cyclical) but also in the variety of your work. "You can work all night and not think about hitting your hours cap on a project that brings you joy or is an investment in a new capability that you want to pitch to other clients. But you will probably have to do some of the boring work that pays the bills. You need to balance what motivates you with being cashflow-positive and to be able to stay afloat through economic cycles," says Gallagher.

CASHFLOW

Speaking of cashflow, this is the hardest part of being a freelancer. Yes, the hourly rate is likely higher than what you made before. But not only are you paying your own taxes and benefits, but you are selling, doing, and invoicing the work. It could be six months from the time you have an idea and get a pitch call with a client to the time you cash the check, and in those six months, you still need to pay sky-high daycare fees and hit the Costco weekly. Kim's advice? "Bill early and bill often. I bill every Friday, like clockwork."

KNOW YOUR VALUE

I am a huge fan of Mika Brzezinksi's book *Know Your Value,* and I recommend everyone read it and use her strategy for determining your market value and negotiating the best deal. And in the world of freelancing, you really need to understand the value of the service you are providing. "Don't give away your best idea in the first one-hour meeting," Kim said. "Twenty years of experience baked that idea in; you need to account for that." How you bill—hourly or as a fixed fee—is dependent upon personal choice and industry norms, but think of this as how large scientific organizations recoup research and development costs. And speaking of billing, consider establishing increments in thirds: at kickoff, at the project midpoint, and at conclusion. This streamlines your invoicing administrative time, gives multiple opportunities for client feedback, and creates predictable cashflow for you.

ANTICIPATE THE COSTS

Besides the obvious costs of home office equipment, taxes, and benefits, there may be some hidden costs that pop up. For instance, as new technology arises, freelancers have to bear the full brunt of costly software license upgrades that larger organizations can spread over a number of employees. Bake those expenses into your rate calculations, but if that's not possible, try to negotiate using your client's equipment or licenses where appropriate.

CARVING OUT TIME—AND PROTECTING IT

You likely chose the freelance approach to have schedule flexibility and a little more control over your day-to-day life. You want to be volunteering at school on Tuesday mornings, and Ringmaster, you now own your schedule, so do it. You can (and will probably have to) bend to client demands most days, but figure out what's most sacred to you and carve it out on your calendar. And if a client meeting pops up for that Tuesday morning? "Sorry," you say confidently. "I have a conflict at that time, would Tuesday afternoon or Wednesday morning work instead?" No need for explanations.

YOU ARE YOUR OWN BRAND

When you work for an organization, you get the coverage of the overall organizational brand, for better or worse. Why should someone hire you for HR Consulting? Because you're part of Mercer, so you must be the best! But when you work for yourself, you are your own brand. Kim elaborates:

When you are freelancing, everything people encounter about you becomes your brand. How you talk, collaborate, problem solve, bill; your presentation style; punctuality, responsiveness, your email signature, your clothing, your car *(not kidding)*, social media, you name it. How you interact with staff on the client side is ultra-important. Many people on staff see freelancers and consultants as "the enemy." We earn more than they do, we have jobs they want, we enjoy a different level of respect. So tread lightly and respectfully, taking time to understand corporate culture and hierarchy and consider no person irrelevant or unimportant. You never know who has whose ear (or is sleeping with whom).

NEVER BURN A BRIDGE

And finally, leave relationships positively and professionally because you will get your next referral from someone you loathe.

RING 2: LIFE

Work doesn't stop when a parent leaves the office. Enter "the second shift." Parents have a whole slew of other tasks to coordinate before they can call it a day. In this section, I will walk you through smarter ways to handle the logistics of life and empower you to do what works best for you and your family. Because the fact is that those little people you created need to eat. *Every single night.*

The mental load, the invisible work of remembering *all the things* for you and your family, is a real thing. It causes high levels of stress and is a main differentiator between working moms and working dads. I don't know why the mental load is carried primarily by moms, even when dad is the primary caregiver, but it is.

I recently delegated "get the twins' sports physicals done" to my husband. It required a delicate dance of scheduling *after* the health insurance premium reset for the free well check but *before* the deadline for player eligibility. It required paperwork to be printed, dropped off, and picked up at the time of appointment to avoid a twenty-five-dollar-times-two fee. But when a question arose on the required paperwork, the nurse at the pediatrician's office called me. Not my husband, who had scheduled the appointment, taken the boys to said appointment, and dropped off said paperwork. "Let me ask you a question," I said in my most respectful voice. "I delegated this chore to my husband. Why are you calling me?"

"Oh, I never call the dads," she said. "They always get it wrong and cause more work for me. Go straight to the moms—that's the best way." Okay, then.

If you're constantly thinking about dinner, after-school activities, or childcare for your family, you're not going to be fully present at your job. In short, you can't rock your job if you're filling out missing camp paperwork, and if you're not rocking your job, you won't get the flexibility you need. You're like those tiny motorcycles in the globe of death. The Ringmaster doesn't need to be the stunt driver going around and around in that metal sphere. There is a better way.

In this section, I empower you, Ringmaster, to be as efficient as possible so that routine life tasks are off your plate and you can focus on being your best self at work. Because here's the dirty little secret of running your circus: if you are rocking the job you have, you will be able to get that flexibility you need, no matter what your corporate policies say. By saying no to more and doing what's right for you and your family (and not what your peers or colleagues say you "have to do") you can streamline the everyday to free you up to kill it at work. And when you are killing it at work, you can demand the flexibility to shine that spotlight wherever it needs to be.

For example, if you have dinner prepped, you might have time for a neighborhood bike ride. If you've got lunches packed the night before and you're not yelling "Hustle!" at your kids, you might have time to throw a football with them a few times in the morning. In this section, I will show you how to prioritize what is important and how to manage (and outsource!) the rest.

CHAPTER 8

MEAL PLANNING (TAMING THE BEASTS)

Traffic was terrible on the way home, your toddler is overtired and hungry at pick up (you know, when they get "hangry"), and your six year-old needs to be at soccer practice at six fifteen. No problem, except that you still have to feed them dinner. Details, details ...

As a parent, you are responsible for satisfying your children's most basic needs, the most consistent of which is food. Meal planning and preparation are ongoing and one of the biggest contributors to your mental load. Between the many food allergies in my house and three growing boys, food gets top billing. Plus, food is more than just fuel; it's a connection point for you and your family. These family connections—especially with your children— are even more important when you're at the office most of the day. But in order for this to happen, you need a plan for shopping and preparing meals.

This chapter talks about planning ahead so that despite your busy life, you are eating something besides circus peanuts for dinner. We will walk through strategies for meal planning, pantry stocking, and sharing the load. It may seem like overkill, but everyone's three-ring circus is a little different *except* when it comes to food. Everyone needs to eat; it's the great equalizer.

MEAL-PLANNING PROCESS

I am going to take it down to a very granular level on what has worked for our family for nearly two decades. We are active folks and big eaters, with whole host of food issues and allergies. Eating good food is very important to me. I find that a simple, healthy meal plan gives me the energy I need to be the Ringmaster I want to be and not fall victim to "hanger." I also find that a well-thought-out meal plan of whole foods has hugely positive mental and physical impacts on my sons, who live with a host of learning challenges. My family spends about as much on food every month as we do our mortgage, but we prioritize good food eaten together as much as possible.

The day of the week and the process may change based on your schedule, but essentially, it's this:

1. On a recurring day of the week, assess what you have in the pantry.

2. Build a meal plan for the week based on what you have and what is on your calendar (i.e., when you will be able to eat together versus evening plans or activities).

3. Make a shopping list of missing ingredients.

4. Prep dinner the night before or morning of, but *never* at dinner time if you can possibly help it.

5. Post the weekly meal plan in a public place (like on the fridge), including that night's dinner directions, so that the first person home (older child, spouse, sitter) can get dinner going at a reasonable hour.

You may be wondering about step 4, not preparing dinner at dinner time. It's counterintuitive, I know, but this may be the most important takeaway for this approach. You've probably got about fifteen minutes in the evening to get dinner on the table before whining turns to squabbling and much worse, which means you can't dice peppers while breaking up a cage match. Dinner must be planned and prepped before you walk in the door.

And believe me, I've learned the hard way. Once, when the twins were seven and my youngest was eighteen months, I put off dinner prep due to a late conference call, and they were cranky and ravenous by the time we sat down at 6:30 p.m. Right then, my cell phone rang, and it was my boss. Trying to prove that I was "always on" and available despite a flexible schedule, I took the call. Not wanting to leave the boys unattended, I let the little guy out of his high chair, placed his tray of uneaten food on the stove top, and begin to dive into whatever was so important that evening. Pretty quickly, I smelled smoke, as I had inadvertently set the plastic high chair tray on a burner that was still on, and yes, I caught the baby's high chair on fire. I hung up the phone and put out the fire, and all was eventually well. But my point is this: they call it the "witching" hour for a reason. After a long day of work and daycare and school, you are all tired and hungry. Dinner has to be ready to go to get you through the evening routine.

Here's how I do it.

On Thursdays, I review grocery store circulars and identify loss leaders, the big-ticket items that grocery stores put on sale each week to draw you in. I then survey the fridge and freezer contents and pantry items, make a list of needed items, and note what meal basics I already have. I then make a meal plan, adding to the list the missing ingredients based on what I have on hand. The meal plan is based on the calendar for the week, so there are no surprises. If there's a Tuesday evening soccer game, I plan for meatball subs and salads to go so we don't eat yet another hot dog concession stand dinner (sorry, marching band boosters). If there's a potluck for the cross-country team on Wednesday, I buy a double pack of tortellini for my pasta salad contribution. The goal here is to minimize the one-off grocery store runs for last-minute items.

On Fridays, I typically knock off a little early and hit the grocery store or have items delivered, leaving a little time for grocery organizing. This includes preparing meat if it needs to be divided and marinated (see tips below) and preparing roughly half of the produce. Every night, after cleaning up the dinner dishes, I pack lunches for me and my husband (when the kids were younger, I packed for them as well), making sure the produce container (aka *"crudité* tray," see below) is stocked with prepped, washed, chopped fruits and veggies, and—here's the key—start to prep the next night's dinner. It might be as simple as pulling out frozen meat or a prepared dish, or I might chop veggies and herbs and even measure out ingredients so that it's easy to throw them together during the witching hours. I supplement this process with monthly runs to Costco and Trader Joe's and weekly trips for in-season produce to the farmer's market. It's a little bit of a luxury, but I have a weekly delivery from a local dairy. From the dairy, we order whole milk, fresh eggs, a pound each of bacon and sausage, and a "farm share bag" of whatever they have in season.

PLAN FOR LEFTOVERS

Unless I have a lunch meeting or date, I bring leftovers and work through lunch. I save money (it's hard to get lunch in D.C. for less than $12!), save the time for fetching lunch, and eat better when I bring my own. And everyone can eat leftovers for weekend lunch. Leftovers can also be used in other meals. Try pork tenderloin—it's super-easy to cook and comes pre-seasoned. Slice up the leftovers for sandwiches during the week. Or try a *completely* foolproof roast chicken. Have roast chicken one night, strip the carcass after dinner, and have the leftovers for a quesadilla later on in the week and chicken salad for lunch. (Don't forget to freeze what's left of the carcass for soup). We had a six-pound, $11 bird a few weeks ago and ate it all week, with the best being homemade chicken noodle soup at the end of the week. Again, I'm no Jacques Pepin, but it's homemade stock from your frozen carcass, chopped-up chicken, and half a box of pasta. That's it.

KEEP IT SIMPLE, BUT NOT *TOO* SIMPLE

We have food allergies and sensitivities, so there's a lot of broiled salmon or grilled chicken, veggies, and fruit. You're not looking for Julia Child here—you're getting dinner on the table. That said, if you make the same three or four meals every week, you and your family are going to be sick of them. "That's it—no more broiled salmon. Call Domino's!" Find a couple of easy resources on the internet or a favorite magazine or newspaper section, and try to add in one new recipe a week to keep food from being boring and to expand your children's palates. Remember—they can't eat chicken nuggets every night if you don't serve them every night. No judgment, just remember that you're in charge. They're not rolling into Kroger on their own to bring those dino nuggets home! You can't stop them from being hungry or snacking between meals, but you are the Ringmaster of your kitchen. Stock it with healthy food.

CRUDITÉ TRAY

The need for healthy, chopped, and prepared fruits and vegetables was born when my children were much younger; apples, celery, carrots, peaches, citrus, everything. I found that if I put the good stuff right in front of them while I made dinner they would be sure to eat their veggies, and I could keep the witching-hour meltdowns at bay. Leave it out during the day and on weekends, and let them graze. It's a good food strategy for young children, but the truth of the matter is that it's just as valuable for the older kids, who are sometimes hungry at different times than normal family mealtimes. One of my teenagers is a big fan of plums, and one recent night, I stopped at the farm stand and bought him a box. He came home from crew practice and ate the entire box in one sitting! Cut and ready-to-eat produce makes it easier for kids to pack their own lunches, and you can easily "grab and go" for healthy snacks at the office. If you're full of the good stuff, it's a lot easier to say no to the cake that mysteriously pops up in the office kitchen several times a week. I serve my *crudités* with hummus, nut butter, or a white bean dip (pureed rinsed and drained cannellini beans with olive oil, salt, and rosemary).

MEAT

Divide and marinate! I typically buy organic meat in bulk from Costco or my local grocer when it is on sale. As soon as you get home from the store, use kitchen scissors to divide a salmon fillet, portions of ground meat, and economy-sized portions of poultry. Pour marinade right in the gallon zipper bag and freeze. Throw Italian or taco seasoning right into your ground beef or turkey. Be sure to label with a Sharpie. The night before, put the bag in the fridge to thaw, and at dinnertime, simply sauté or grill a pre-prepped meal, or throw the meat on a sheet pan with vegetables for the easiest weeknight dinner (see below).

COOK ON SUNDAYS AND DOUBLE UP

Make your most complicated meal on the weekend when your spouse is home to mind the little ones so you're not breaking up sibling squabbles while trying to double recipe ingredients in your head. Speaking of doubling, if you make a meatloaf, make two. Double your batch of turkey chili. Freeze the second. It doesn't take any more time to double than to make a single, and you'll have something in the freezer later on for busy weeknights. Make a large batch of a grain like rice or quinoa on the weekend to use in multiple meals. Make a base of a "big salad" (hard veggies plus washed and chopped greens), and then quickly add meat and toppings for a dinner or lunch salad.

SHEET PAN DINNERS

While I am a big fan of my electric pressure cooker and lay claim to four different slow cookers (c'mon! I need all the different sizes!), the most helpful kitchen device is the humble sheet pan. I have a half dozen, nothing fancy, and they are the workhorses that make easy weeknight dinners possible. Prep is organized, and cleanup is limited to one or two pans.

While the internet abounds with delicious recipes, the basics here are as follows: Thaw marinated meat, add prepped veggies, and cover with foil the night before. Write cooking instructions on foil with a Sharpie permanent marker (for example, "Preheat oven to 350 degrees, cook 35 minutes, flipping once. Save some for mom!"). Your child will be extremely proud of himself when he becomes responsible enough to "make" dinner for the family by simply popping it in the oven.

Always make another pan of roast veggies, slicing for maximum exposure to the sheet pan (e.g. cut cauliflower into steaks instead of florets) to get that crunchy brown crust. Toss with olive or avocado oil, salt, and pepper, and you will have extra veggies for breakfast, lunch bowls, or other meals. I am a huge fan of reheating roast veggies in the morning with a runny egg or two. It takes me from post-morning-workout all the way through lunch without snacking on the junk in the office kitchen.

BUS STOP MEAL SWAP

Now I am really going to blow your mind. For four years during the meaty part of the elementary school phase, chock-full of evening sports and scout commitments, three other families of five at my bus stop formed a weeknight meal swap. Each night, Monday through Thursday, one of us cooked for twenty (four families of five!) and handed off meals at the 4 p.m. bus stop. I applied all of my management consulting process improvement know-how to the simple fact that all four families were trying to do the impossible: get dinner on the table after a long workday when the evenings were a logistical nightmare.

And there were secondary benefits, too. My kids (and I!) were exposed to a lot of new and different foods. Things I didn't know (or care to know) how to make and food from other cultures. This put the kibosh on picky eating; "This is it for dinner. If you don't like it, you may wait until breakfast." And there was no greater joy than a small child hopping off the bus to learn that "Ofa's ribs" or "Gina's roast" was for dinner.

Three of the four moms worked outside the home, and the fourth had two kids under two at the time, so this was not about being hipper-than-thou, healthier meal prep, or cost savings; it was more about the logistics of getting dinner on the table at 5:30 p.m. when dance class is at 6:00 p.m. and dad isn't home until 7:00 p.m. (thank you, rush hour). Cook one night (or the night before—my average time commitment was around ninety minutes) for twenty, and the rest of the week, hot dinner is delivered. Find your people, and suggest a trial run of the meal swap. Because when it works, it's genius.

AND LASTLY, THE CLEAN-OUT MEAL

Every Friday night is leftover buffet at our house. We often have extra kids or neighbors milling about, and I simply take out all the food and say, "Have at it 'til it's gone!" Lay out all of the leftover bits, along with a variety of dressings and sauces for create-your-own dinner success. Serve it with chopsticks or toothpicks, bread chunks, or whatever it takes to clean out the fridge, because tomorrow you will start the cycle all over again.

WHAT'S IN A HEALTH EDUCATOR'S PANTRY?

I sat down with Mai Trihn, busy working mother of three and a health educator at MaiHealthNow.com, to see what was in her pantry and how she approached the daily grind of getting everyone fed with good food.

WHAT EXACTLY IS A HEALTH EDUCATOR?

I am a certified health counselor and chronic disease prevention expert. And the first line of attack is nutrition. If you put water in a gas tank, it doesn't drive. You can't put crappy food in your body. Food is your fuel.

YOU HAVE THREE ACTIVE KIDS AND A THRIVING PRACTICE. HOW DO YOU GET DINNER ON THE TABLE EVERY NIGHT?

Look, I was single for six years. We had to keep it simple. We don't do soda or fast food. But I use the crockpot many nights of the week, and we always have frozen vegetables with a little butter on them. It's fast or ready when we get home. We stick to simple meals like whole wheat quesadillas with vegetarian refried beans and something fresh like cantaloupe. We don't eat a lot of refined carbs, and if we do, it's something like quinoa pasta. If you're eating carbs, check the fiber—that's what cleans your system from junk. Three-bean turkey chili is a winner.

HOW DO YOU HANDLE THE INEVITABLE TREATS? DO YOU HAVE TO BE THE "TREAT POLICE?"

I go with the 80/20 rule. We eat only good food at home, so I don't stress out about treat food at parties. The only big rule is no soda. And they need to learn how to make good choices. They live in the real world; they *will* have hamburgers at a pool cookout.

CHAPTER 9

SHARING THE LOAD

There's a lot happening under the big top of your three-ring circus. And if you're following along, you know that the key to maintaining some semblance of order is to decide what goes in each ring and where the spotlight shines. When it comes to sharing the load, each family must decide who is in charge of what, play to each partner's strengths, and not micromanage each other. This assumes, of course, that a partner is involved. Families come in all shapes and sizes, and there are single parents and partners who can't (or won't) share the load equally. These scenarios require extra support and village-building.

Get four moms together over a bottle of wine and take bets on how long it takes for the first woman to say her husband isn't doing enough. Get four dads together over a bottle of whiskey and take bets on many glasses are downed before the first guy says his wife is "overcommitted with volunteer activities, stressed out, and worrying about all these crazy little things."

You have way too much to do to keep score.
You need to divide and conquer.

A while back, I looked over at my husband, who was doing his normal dinner dish duty cleanup for the meal I had prepared while I shifted to breakfast prep and lunch packing and said, "Did we ever actually *talk* about this? Or did we just fall into natural roles when it comes to sharing the load?"

"We just do what needs to get done," he said.

And while we've mostly been able to share the load equally, we've struggled when it comes to transitions. When one of us has taken on a bigger role or more work travel and the other has to pick up more of the share, tempers flare. Or when school or work schedules shift and so must responsibilities, it's easy to start keeping score. But you have *way* too much to do to keep score. You need to divide and conquer.

You need to have a come-to-Jesus meeting about what needs to be done and how you're going to do it. Get out a pen and paper and write down everything that needs to be done. All of it. The big, the small. The major and the mundane. But you have to first agree on "what needs to be done." Overflowing dresser drawers may be making you nuts, but if your spouse doesn't care, "cleaning out clothes" cannot go on this list. Focus on the recurring tasks, evaluate interests and strengths (and perhaps most importantly, strong distastes), and divide and conquer. Like the financial theory to "ignore sunk costs," don't worry about who did what in the past. Or that you've packed lunches for eleven years without sufficient credit. Focus instead on what needs to happen *today, right now*. Write down all of the must-dos and figure out an equitable way to share the load.

These negotiations can be fraught with all sorts of baggage, so navigate this minefield carefully. Whether we like it or not, our cultural customs and familial experiences lead us toward gender norms and biases. Maybe your husband's mother stayed home full-time, and he never saw his father change a diaper. Or perhaps you never learned to cook, which is just fine with you, but unfortunately, the wee beasts demand dinner each night. A female executive colleague once told me the story of her southeast Asian mother-in-law decrying her husband's kitchen work. "My Harvard-educated son, emptying the dishwasher? Where have I gone wrong?" As hard as it is, try to remove emotion from the equation and simply be pragmatic about it. You, your spouse, and the kids all need to get to work/school/daycare. You need to get home at night. You need to eat, bathe, wear clean clothes, and maybe read a story or two. The rest? That's negotiable.

Let's talk about the big stuff.

PICKUP/DROP OFF

Evaluate schedules so that—if possible—no one parent is doing both pickup and drop-off, providing both before- and after-school care, or being the only one relieving the babysitter. In our household, the compromise is that my husband works from home on Mondays and Thursdays so that I can be in the office for my weekly early morning management team meetings. On the three days per week he is in the office, he needs to be at his desk by 7:30 a.m., so I do the morning shuffle. But that morning shuffle means that I'm not at my desk until nine thirty or later, which makes for a later return home, and he's on dinner and evening duty.

One of you may have a work location or schedule inflexibility that requires the other to do both morning and evening routines. If that's the case, figure out where you can hit the pressure release valve on other responsibilities. For example, if daycare is near your office, making it most feasible for you to do both drop-off and pickup, perhaps your husband can have dinner waiting when you get home (or at least have it prepped, to ward off the witching-hour meltdowns).

HOUSECLEANING

Hopefully you've ironed at least some of this out pre-kids, but kids are wild animals and come with an incredible ability to mess the place up. When we moved out of our house several years ago for a major renovation, I packed up the dining room and noticed a giant tomato sauce stain. Wondering when and how that happened, I asked my husband if he knew anything about it. "Oh that?" he asked. "It's been there for years."

If you can—and this isn't a luxury affordable for everyone—get some help in the form of a regular housekeeper. It's one of the easiest tasks to outsource completely and can significantly improve your lifestyle, increase your time with your family, and lower the tension with your partner. When you have a housekeeper, you get the added benefit (or consequence, depending on whom you ask) of "cleaning up for the housecleaner." But if boys don't want legos moved, they must first be in a bin. If my husband's bookkeeping duties have papers and bills strewn about, he must organize and deal with them before these saints come in and make order of our world.

We have gone through many a tight budget cycle but have—for the most part—prioritized housekeeping expenses above others like vacations and cable. My stress level is simply lower when there is less clutter and the bathrooms don't smell like train stations.

DISTRIBUTING THE EFFORT

Even if you are able to afford some outside help, running a household is a tremendous task. The "second shift" is for real, and it often comes on the heels of a long workday. Here are some tips for lightening the load.

MAN UP, KIDS

I have no idea why we say "man up" when it's clear to just about everyone that women are the stronger sex, but alas, the kids have to step it up. Kids can do more at younger ages than we think, and while it may take a while to teach the younger set, and they certainly won't do it as well as you can, they have to contribute. Think of it as training young analysts at work. Yes, it's easier and faster if you make that pitch deck yourself, but that's not the point. Your job is to teach them so that they can eventually do their share.

BASIC RULES

Chore charts never worked for our family. They always seemed like more management work for me, and running kids' allowances became more tedious than my own financial planning and analysis work. Instead, we came up with some basic family rules. Remember—I rule the Folsom Frat House (see Epilogue for the 100% true Folsom House Rules), so I've had to lower my standards substantially. But establishing basic human decency ground rules has been extremely helpful. Hang up wet towels. Shoes and backpacks go in cubbies. Rinsed dishes go in the dishwasher. If you see a full trash can, take it out to the bin. And because I live in a boy house, wipe down the bathroom every night with a Clorox wipe. But the messy teenage boy rooms? I just shut the door. Not a fight I choose to pick.

SIMPLIFY

My graduate school process and operations professor used to preach that the "key to efficiency is to reduce variability." I scrapped the mismatch of linens and socks—the bane of my laundry existence—for the same sets of white sheets, towels, and basic gym socks. They come clean with bleach, no matter what trauma has befallen them at the hands of my boys, and require no matching.

MINIMIZE

Back to the overflowing drawers analogy, because it really drives me nuts. Overflowing drawers also make it really hard to keep a room clean and get clean laundry put away. And the thing that drives me mad is clean laundry sitting around, not put away, and dirty little boys living out of a clean laundry basket. Applying my process operations management skills, I figured out that the bottleneck is the drawer stuffed with too-small clothes. For me, it's worth it to spend thirty minutes with each child each season to eliminate what is stained, too small, or just "not my favorite" for the hand-me-down or donation pile so that even a four year old can put her own laundry away and make a clothes shopping list for the next season. If you are blessed to be on the receiving end of hand-me-downs, cull through that garbage bag the day it appears on your doorstep, lest it sit in a closet for months, your child bypassing the size or season entirely. Pull out anything you won't use, and store the rest by clearly-marked size in a small tub or Super XL Ziploc bag under a bed or in the closet. And while I aspire to a "capsule closet" approach for all of us, the reality is that they don't need that many clothes. You're already doing laundry every day; keep it simple and pared down.

INCENTIVIZE

While most people appreciate a clean house, very few enjoy the actual cleaning part. With younger kids, try very short-term incentives. If the dishes are loaded, lunches packed, and rooms picked up, you can have thirty minutes of screen time. Or take a page from the book of a marketing executive friend who felt her four children weren't quite doing enough around the house at a time when they were going through a financial transition. She fired the housekeeper, made a complete house cleaning chart for the siblings to tackle collaboratively (each picking two items so it was fair), and she used the housekeeper dollars for fun family outings like theme parks and dinners out. Brilliant.

MEAL PREP AND CLEANUP

While every family dynamic is unique, the one thing we have in common is that we all need to eat. Every single day, you and the wee beasts must prepare, consume, and clean up multiple meals. How you handle this monumental, daily task is largely up to your own familial priorities, but you need a plan. I'm always amazed when a friend with kids says, "Oh, it's six thirty—no wonder the kids are cranky. I guess I need to figure out what I'm going to make for dinner!" At six thirty? No way, Jose. That ship has sailed. Chapter 8 covered meal planning in detail, but I think it's important to share the load here, as it's such a large and ongoing family task. In our house, if one cooks, the other cleans up. I am good at meal planning, so I play to my strengths there and do most of the food shopping. If that task needs to be handed off due to other work obligations like travel, a strong meal plan means a detailed list is all but auto-generated.

As soon as the children are able, have them pack their own lunches. I waited far too long to make this a requirement and got resentful when I discovered thrown-away or uneaten lunches. You buy good food; they pack it. The end.

LAUNDRY

I keep trying to reach "laundry nirvana," where all clothes save the ones on your bodies are clean, washed, and put away. But as an active family of five, such a place does not exist. In our house, the three appliances guaranteed to be used every single day are, in this order: coffee maker, washer, and dryer.

Successful load sharing (get it? Mom joke!) of laundry requires its own set of negotiations. You both agree it needs to get done, but how? If your partner cares more about, say, overflowing laundry baskets, are you willing to do a load a day, rather than a Sunday marathon with all of your friends from the Bravo network? And this is not the place to micromanage. I'm sure you are better at laundry and have never created something-red-in-the-washer pink t-shirts or shrunk a wool sweater, but the potential for loss is not as great as the time and stress saved by sharing the laundry load. You can buy a new sweater; you can't get back that hour on Sunday.

Until recently, I took the all-in approach to laundry. We had some basic rules: when your basket is full, bring it to the laundry. Everyone sorts, folds, and puts away their own laundry. But my husband I were doing one to two loads per day. As the boys have gotten older, I have shifted to having each of them do their own from start to finish. As crazy as this sounds, I think there are some important lessons to learn, particularly around the area of executive functioning. This isn't about clean clothes; it's about raising future functional adults. If I have a game today and tomorrow, I need to wash my own uniform tonight. If I go to school and leave my clothes in the washer all day, they will smell disgusting even after they come out of the dresser drawer. If I leave my clothes in the dryer for two days, my brother, with whom I share laundry facilities, will probably dump my clean clothes in a pile on the floor. Thinking about how the whole process fits together is a step—I hope—toward functional, clean-clothed adulthood.

This isn't about clean clothes; it's about raising future functional adults.

SICK DAYS, SNOW DAYS, AND ALL THE DAMNED MEDICAL APPOINTMENTS

Just as dinner every night shouldn't come as a surprise, neither should sick or snow (or inclement weather of choice) days. Like death and taxes, your working parenthood will collide with a child getting sick or daycare closing for a polar vortex or heat dome or incoming floods. To avoid the 6 a.m. grudge match, agree how you will handle these in advance. You can agree to evaluate based on your own individual workday schedule for each event, or one takes sick and the other takes snow. Either way, you need a plan.

The other certainty is that kids have *lots* of medical appointments. And all of them will happen while you and your spouse are supposed to be at work. If each child has a pediatrician and dentist, you're guaranteed two to four appointments per year per child. Throw in an orthodontist, optometrist, and a speech or occupational therapist, and you're basically the medical version of an Uber driver.

In our own division of labor, my husband (with near-unlimited sick leave) takes broken bones and dentist. With my schedule flexibility, I cover pediatric well checks and specialists. We tag team on the three-step process to get and fill monthly prescriptions. No matter your division of labor, prioritize dentists with evening hours, pediatricians with early walk-in hours, and any provider within a three-mile radius of your home.

FINANCES

In a two-working parent household, you're both responsible for the money you bring in and how you spend it. Luckily, most of the inflows and outflows are set day to day and month to month. But you still need to agree on big-ticket items like how much you're going to spend on housing and food and whether it's time for a new car or how to pay for a vacation. Try to sit down once a year and evaluate all inflows, outflows, and large planned expenditures (like new cars or big vacations), and try to cut expenses by 10 percent to prevent spend creep. Detailed budgets, like a strict diet, have never worked for me. Instead, I advocate for agreeing on the big stuff and letting the rest go. Covering expenses and saving for emergencies, retirement, and college? Great. I don't need to know about my husband's daily shipment of low-dollar vintage bike parts, and he doesn't give me the Spanish inquisition for my oat milk latte habit. If one partner does the bill paying, perhaps the other does the "big" stuff like taxes and investments. No single partner should hold all the cards.

THE MENTAL LOAD

While we have covered many of the traditional "big stuff" items, the mental load is where the trains sometimes come off the rails. I resist gross gender-based generalizations, but on the main, I find that women are very strong at keeping all of the details in their heads. Again with the generalization, but with a limited ability to compartmentalize, we understand how things fit together. This emotional intelligence is what makes us tremendous leaders in the workplace, but it can cause freak-outs (that's a technical term!), feeling overwhelmed, and, ultimately, burnout.

The week before I left work for sabbatical, I was in a major presentation with a C-level client. It was also the week my teenagers were interviewing for summer jobs. Sensing this collision of hazards, I asked my husband, who was working at home the day of the interviews, to take over. Full stop. I needed to nail this presentation and leave work on a high note.

Predictably, during the presentation, I received a number of texts: "Where are the birth certificates? What's my social security number? What's *his* social security number?" Unsuccessful at answering the texts under the conference room table, I stepped out to the "ladies' room" (code word for going to the stall and screaming into my cell phone, *"I cannot be the only person who holds this information!"*). Stressed and angry about my less-than-professional presentation, I read the riot act to my entire family about this. My seventeen-year-old son very calmly said, "Mom, I've only needed to know my own social security number once before. I didn't memorize it last year from my employment paperwork. Can you teach it to me?" Ugh. Straight to the heart. I drilled his phone number and home address into his head when he was four; why didn't I drill this key piece of information for future adulthood?

Despite careful planning, you will experience mental overload as you juggle all of the balls of your three-ring circus. To lighten the load, I share these simple, practical, but often overlooked tips so your brain doesn't have to be the holder of all of the information:

DAYCARE AND SCHOOL CONTACT INFORMATION

Make sure primary contact information isn't only one parent, namely you. A couple of years ago, I was on a high-profile business trip and received an email from my son's fourth grade teacher with the subject line "Flatulence." Never mind the hilarity of the topic; she chose to reach out to me first, not my husband, who was working from home two blocks from the school and could have much more easily handled whatever GI-based problem there was at school that day. When I asked her why she chose me, she said, "Your name was first on the contact list." Lesson learned.

FORMS

I often wonder how children ever became adults in a time before forms. There are forms for every school year, camp, sports league, dance season, and religious education registration, and even annual form updates at each of the aforementioned medical providers. As soon as they are able, as young as eight, have children complete part or all of these forms. This is how they memorize their social security numbers, so as not to cause a complete meltdown while you are trying to give a major presentation. And you minimize your carpal tunnel syndrome; win-win. And if your kids are too small to do this, have your spouse do his or her fair share of the form-filling-outing. My guess is that your spouse's number will go first in the contact list. Double win!

GROUP TEXTS FOR BUS STOP/DAYCARE PICKUP

At the beginning of the year, create a group text titled "Bus Stop Pickup" and share it with your spouse. Include the contact information of anyone at your bus stop, or authorized daycare picker-uppers, who could put on a cape and save the day with a quick "Stuck in tunnel traffic. Can you pick up Emily at the bus?" text.

SCAN AND SAVE KEY DOCS

Prevent the last-minute scramble accompanying said forms and save all of your key documents to a private, password-protected shared drive. I like Dropbox, but use what works for you. I keep social security cards, birth certificates, annual medical exams, and vaccine history for each child for smooth sailing through registration.

SINGLE PARENTHOOD

Whether by choice or circumstances, there are single parents out there who are making all the things work every single day. They are my heroes. I turned to successful single mother of two adult daughters and chief of staff at World Food Program USA, Shannon Hiskey, to share her advice. She has gone through the struggle and come out on the other side.

WHEN YOU HAVE NO ONE WITH WHOM TO SHARE THE LOAD, HOW DO YOU GET IT ALL DONE?

Time management is paramount—and also oddly empowering. Comprehensive list-making, pre-planning, and strong adherence to calendars have been the keys to my survival. Also, checking things off of a list can bring a welcome sigh of relief as well as a sense of accomplishment.

WHAT DO YOU DO TO FIGHT THE FEELING OF BEING OVERWHELMED?

Journaling! "Me time" is key, and it is helpful to get my thoughts out on paper before they come across the wrong way to the wrong person at the wrong time. A major benefit to journaling is to be able to refer back to previous concerns or challenges and see what I have successfully overcome—or not.

HOW HAVE YOU ADDRESSED THIS WITH YOUR WORK? DO YOUR MANAGER AND COLLEAGUES KNOW YOU'RE SINGLE? HOW IS YOUR SINGLE STATUS PERCEIVED?

I am beyond grateful to work in an environment where "family first" is the motto. But this was not the case when my children were toddlers, or when I was racing to and from the office sometimes two or three times daily for school meetings or events, soccer practice, or midday medical appointments. Cultivating honest relationships with colleagues and managers is important to building support and understanding for one another. While fellow employees may or may not be single parents, most likely they are coping with some significant life "thing" while managing a hectic work schedule.

HOW DO YOU HANDLE WORK TRAVEL?

Arranged sleepovers with other families. It's fun for the kids and makes the guilt seem less weighty.

HOW DO YOU BUILD YOUR VILLAGE?

I was very close to moving far away after my mother passed away suddenly during my divorce (my ex-husband had moved to another state) because I desperately wanted a fresh start. However, I decided that continuity was nearly all that was left for my children and myself. Staying close to neighbors and my preschool playgroup/soccer/ballet moms and getting a new job in an energetic environment were life-saving for me emotionally—and provided stability for my girls. I've lived in our home for twenty-five years now, where I've raised both of my adult daughters as a single mom.

WHAT'S THE BEST PIECE OF ADVICE YOU COULD SHARE WITH OTHER SINGLE WORKING MAMAS OUT THERE GETTING IT DONE?

Trust your gut. You know yourself and your children better than anyone. And someone once told me they'd rather hire someone with life experience than with a long list of degrees. Life experience makes you more well-rounded, a terrific problem-solver, and compassionate—all great traits to make a great leader. Wear it like the badge you've earned!

A word of caution about sharing the load: mind the transitions. If you get that big promotion (yay, you!), you probably can't continue to do drop-off and pickup. If your hours get cut and your husband is on the grind trying to make a bigger-than-normal bonus to make up for the shortfall, you are probably doing dinner duty every night while he works late. My point is this is never solved. It's always evolving. Your work changes. His or her work changes. The kids' school scheduled changes. This isn't about score-keeping. It's about figuring out what needs to be done and sharing the load. The rest is icing on the cake.

CHAPTER 10

PUMPING

Pumping applies only to a small segment of readers, the women who choose and are able to breastfeed, and for a very short portion of motherhood. But boy howdy, is it a lot of work and a logistics nightmare for working moms!

I will go to my grave saying that breastfeeding infant premature twin boys was the hardest thing I've ever done. I had to pump exclusively for six weeks before they even began to latch, and only with the help of an expensive-but-talented lactation consultant were we able to get the hang of it. I fought so hard to get it right that I didn't want to drop it entirely when I went back to work after six months. But I was working as a management consultant on a client site, a military installation, without any dedicated pumping facilities. My choices were to pump in the stall of a bathroom or to ask my client to leave his office, the one we shared, so I could pump. New to the workforce as a mom, I just didn't have the confidence to do it. So I dropped to nursing before and after work and made it to nine months before we all gave up. With dedicated facilities and a solid pumping plan, I might have been able to make it to the one-year mark recommended by the American Academy of Pediatrics.

Luckily, the US has made significant strides in promoting and supporting pumping among new mothers in the workforce. States and cities have enacted policies to encourage and support breastfeeding moms, and companies have realized that this is but a tiny expense for "breaks" (ha!) and space to attract and retain their top talent.

But it is still a ton of work, and work only you can do. While you can't delegate this work, or share the load, you can enlist your support team to make sure this relatively short but logistically challenging phase is successful.

EQUIPMENT

I strongly recommend you purchase *really* good pumping equipment. Some insurance plans will subsidize the cost, but overall, this is where you want to spend a good chunk of your post-baby budget. Yes, the baby clothes are adorable, but they will be in and out of them in a month. Spend your money on a good pump that will be comfortable and efficient and get you through a tough logistical period. And it's a lot less than formula over that same time period (and my boys always had supplemental formula; this isn't a judgment—it's about allocation of limited post-baby resources).

HUMAN RESOURCES AND MANAGER

About a month before your return to work, schedule a meeting with your manager and human resources department to discuss plans for a location to pump and store breast milk in the office. Read your employee handbook in advance so you know what the policies are, as well as state and local regulations around nursing and pumping. Also, seek out other women who have successfully done this. Ask human resources to connect you with someone if no one like this already exists in your network.

SUPPORT

Larger organizations have breastfeeding support groups, and for good reason. They are one of the largest indicators of retention among mothers returning to work. Seek out this group and join. If it's not your scene, no problem, but these folks may just become your people. And you are going to need your people, as you will read in chapter 12, "Building Your Village." And if your office doesn't have this support group, seek out external support groups. It's a very defined period of time, and you will need the support of women who know what you are going through right this very moment. A United States Senate staffer friend told me that one of the few places on Capitol Hill where women could agree on most things was the Senate nursing moms' support group.

SCHEDULE AND LOGISTICS

Block time on your calendar when you need to pump and hold that time as sacred. You can let those closest to you know what "blocked" on your calendar means, but you don't owe that explanation to anyone else. You are simply not available for meetings at that time. Read emails, review documents, or just chill out. You'll need it. If you travel regularly, download the airport app to locate pumping facilities in advance so that you are not running to the gate in pain. Determine whether your company will pay for shipped milk while you travel via services like Milk Stork. If you attend conferences in meeting facilities, call ahead to see what their lactation room options are. You know you will need to pump every three hours; just plan that right into your day.

And moms, if you don't pump, you're still a great mom. As my dear lactation consultant told me, if it's too much stress to pump, you're negating the benefits because you're passing that stress on to your child. If this works for you, great. If not, get a great bottle brush and just go with it.

KAYE BURTON, MANAGER AND MOM OF THREE UNDER THREE

As my own experience pumping is, ahem, a bit dated, I turned to my colleague and supermom rock star Kaye Burton for her advice on pumping. Kaye had infant twins when her oldest was twenty months old. That's right, three boys under three. And she came back to work full-time following both maternity leaves and knocked it out of the park.

WHAT ARE YOUR BEST TIPS TO SHARE FOR WORKING MOMS AND PUMPING?

Pumping honestly *sucks*. I literally had a countdown on my homepage that listed the number of days until I could stop pumping with the twins, so even though I successfully made it to a year or more each time, it was not something that was easy for me. I remember when I made the switch from three times per day to twice daily, it felt *so* amazing, like I got so much of my life back. Even though it feels very lonely, like no one can relate to you (especially if you work in an office with lots of men or people without kids), the pumping phase is a relatively short one, and you will get through it. I always had a goal to make it to one year nursing because that was the recommendation from my pediatrician, but also because formula is so darned expensive (especially with twins). However, it also doesn't have to be all or nothing. You can always cut back on pumping a little bit. Just having that option in the back of my head really took the pressure off quite a bit.

HOW DID YOU HANDLE WORK BREAKS?

Set appointments on your calendar and try to stick to them. You can move them around for important meetings, but don't skip them entirely; otherwise, you may get into the habit of skipping, and your supply will suffer. If colleagues ask where you're going, just tell them you're going to a meeting and that you'll be back in thirty minutes.

Try to create a space where you can work while you're pumping— bring in a table with enough space to put your pump and laptop on so that you can work while pumping. When I was working at a hectic client site, these thirty-minute breaks were often some of my most productive parts of the day. But I also used those times to take a few minutes to look at pictures or videos of my kids—this is especially helpful if you have supply issues or issues with pumping in general because thinking about your baby can help stimulate letdown.

HOW DID YOU HANDLE WORK TRAVEL?

Travel was tough, but luckily, I have coworkers whom I am comfortable with so that I can tell them why I need to take a twenty-to-thirty-minute break from our schedule every few hours. Logistically, planning ahead is key. Call the conference staff or hotel concierge in advance to make sure they have a lactation facility. Schedule your travel to allow time for pumping. If you have frequent travel, consider investing in a second cordless pump. I have also pumped in a lot of unfortunate places, such as in a bathroom in the Miami airport when no one could tell me where the "lactation pod" was located, and in the bathrooms on *many* Amtrak trains. Bring lots of paper towels and plastic storage bags to keep pump accessories away from gross surfaces and to use as emergency ice packs if travel keeps you away from a fridge for a long while.

HOW DO YOU MAKE SURE YOU'RE TAKING CARE OF YOU (GOOD FOOD, HYDRATION) WHILE WORKING, PUMPING, AND COMING HOME TO A SECOND SHIFT OF INFANT CARE?

I would bring my giant water bottle to my pump sessions, filling it up on the way and finishing it during my session. I always had a huge appetite while nursing, so I had tons of snacks on hand at all times. I would often eat breakfast when I got to work and then a snack before lunch and a snack (or two or three) before dinner. Snacks were often granola bars or protein bars for me, since they are so easy to grab and go and can be kept in your work bag or at your desk, but I'm also a big fan of yogurt, fruit, and cheese sticks.

No matter how you decide to feed your baby, you are an amazing mom. But the logistics around nursing and pumping, particularly with painfully short (if any) new parent leave policies in the United States, require extra planning and support. It is quite literally the one thing you can't outsource, but you can absolutely enlist the support of your partner and colleagues to help reach your pumping goal.

RING 3: YOU

Well, Ringmaster, you've finally arrived at Ring 3. This is all about you, the sweet spot that intersects your work and life rings. This is where it all comes together; where the magic happens. It's all about the mindset, and the Ringmaster is in control. Now that you have Rings 1 (Work) and 2 (Life) somewhat under control, you have the opportunity to live a more intentional, less stressful life. You are your own Ringmaster, and you decide what goes into each ring and where the spotlight shines. And that spotlight moves *all* the time! It'll change from day to day, hour to hour, but that's okay. Your life is a circus, and it's *hard,* but you don't have to succumb to society's standards on how to live and work. This is about you. Your family. Your life.

The big idea is to focus on decisions, not reactions. To live an intentional life that works for you, you have to make decisions about you, your work, and your family that may not always be popular. Life is about decisions, and you need to feel empowered to do what's right for you, not what you feel like you *ought* to be doing.

For example, early on, I made a conscious decision to intercept most preschool birthday party invitations my children received and regretfully decline most of them. I knew that my kids wouldn't remember most of their preschool friends, and I didn't want to devote every Saturday afternoon to Chuck E. Cheese (codename: *Charles A Fromage* in our house). In order to keep it all together, you will have to make some very specific decisions about you and your family and how you want to live your lives.

Let's learn how.

CHAPTER 11

EXERCISE

Look, Ringmaster. I'm not here to shame you into exercising. Rather, I'm here to convince you in some form or fashion that you need to do this. It's about wellness and stress management and moving your body. I want to offer you strategies on how to make it happen when I know that you are already twirling multiple batons.

There's a reason the "you" ring starts with exercise. A regular fitness routine will give you much-needed energy, will reduce stress (and sister, you are *stressed* out right now), and will set a strong example for children. I've managed to keep exercise a constant for seventeen years of full-time work with three kids. If I can figure it out, you can too. There is no magic here. I'm not special. I made it a priority and got creative. And you can, too.

Exercise has always been part of my daily routine, but as I get older, it's becoming even more of a priority. When my twins were very young, I would leave work at 4:00 p.m., relieve the nanny, and schlep the boys to the nursery at the local gym. I felt guilt about trading one care strategy for another, and it was typically the very last thing I wanted to do in the evening, but I knew it was critical for me—at least twice a week—to crank up some tunes and go for an hour on a cardio machine, or lift heavy weights to build and maintain muscle.

Funny thing about Father Time: he just keeps on ticking. And as my children—and I—have gotten older, my own fitness routine has evolved into the basis of my self-care practice. I find that morning workouts are key, even if you're not a morning person. There's just too much that can go wrong by the end of the day, and it's too easy to push off a workout. I run or work out three mornings a week with girlfriends in the neighborhood; it's my only dedicated, recurring social time. I lift weights at the office gym on Thursday mornings (before my management team meeting) and for the last decade have played on an "old lady" soccer team on Saturday mornings. Despite what the little bosses may think, life is not all about the kids. On Saturdays when their own games don't conflict, I insist they cheer for *me* on the sidelines. And I know life is better if I can get in at least one yoga class per week. You need to find the right mix of much-needed social time, alone time, and body movement that works for you.

Ringmaster, I want to motivate you to bypass the snooze button. I want you to figure out what makes your mind and body happy and to create a sustainable plan that works for you. Make an exercise date for yourself, the only time all day that's just for you. Make it a priority; put it on the calendar. Don't cancel. The keys to long-term success are accountability with friends, prioritization in your schedule, and variety to keep it interesting.

REMEMBER WHY YOU'RE DOING IT

This isn't about vanity, Ringmaster. You're long past needing to fit into your skinny jeans just to feel good about yourself. This is about managing your stress, giving you energy, and modeling an active lifestyle for your children. If you can remember the "why," you are less likely to cancel a power walk date with a friend or skip yoga class. And if you fall off the exercise wagon, the worst thing you can do is to stay sedentary. Start somewhere, anywhere, and move your body. You will never say, "Gosh I'm glad I hit the snooze button this morning and skipped my workout."

FIND YOUR PEOPLE

You've all read the research that partners in accountability—more than any other single factor—indicate success in a long-term change like starting and maintaining a fitness plan. But what you really need to do is just find your people. They will keep you motivated, and you'll have more fun doing it. And if you're having fun doing it, you will *keep* doing it.

I started running years ago with some of the ladies in my neighborhood in the early morning, hours before kids were up and spouses departed for work. Safety in numbers: we donned reflective vests and headlamps as we set out at 5:30 a.m. for the various routes we had mapped out. Even when it's twenty degrees in February, it's hard to say "Nah, too cold" when your BFFs are waiting for you on the corner. We would train together for a couple of races each year, including a couple of fun destinations for a girlfriends' trip. That became my only regular social time, and a heck of a lot healthier than catching up with them over drinks (though we did that, too).

But things really heated up when, on a random weekday pre-dawn run, a woman approached us and said, "Hey, y'all look nice, mind if I run with you?" From there, we formed the "Group Text Running Club" and took wellness to a whole new level. We have daily check-ins on step count, share photos of beautiful, healthy meals, and encourage daily meditation practices. It's become a virtuous cycle. We encourage each other to eat a little healthier, stay hydrated, drink a little less alcohol, and sleep a little more so that we can do more hanging out while moving our bodies. Win-win-win.

If you're not lucky enough to live within blocks of wonderful but crazy friends who will get up with you in the predawn hours several times a week and keep you honest, use existing networks to find your people. Join a martial arts studio. Find a "Moms on the Run" chapter in your zip code, like the one I run (ha! Another mom joke!) into weekly at the high school track. Go on a yoga retreat to meet fellow yogis in your area. You have to put yourself out there, as my friend did.

And don't overlook the value of some alone time. One of my dear friends likes to do races with our group, but she wants to run alongside us with headphones on while we gab away. Running is her quiet, alone time. And that's fine! You do you! I can walk for miles with a good audiobook or podcast, and sometimes that's just the right thing for me.

DO THE RIGHT THING

I came to running later in life, completing my first 10K while six months pregnant with my third son. A lifelong soccer player, I never had "real" running coaching. And what training and nutrition advice I received in my teens and twenties certainly didn't hold water in my thirties and forties.

I noticed a weird thing that kept happening. The harder and longer I worked out, the hungrier I was. I know what you're thinking: *Duh.* But every time I trained for a race with a dedicated training plan, I gained weight. Despite eating what I thought was healthy food and exercising more, I was getting further away from my fitness goals. Not sure what was happening, I turned to trainer and nutrition coach Leslie Ann Quillen of Fat Loss Lifestyle for advice. You can read more from Leslie Ann in the callout box, but from her I learned that "static cardio"—that is, going for a five-or-six-mile run or spending an hour on the elliptical at a steady rate—actually has the reverse effect. You're hungrier, not "tricking" your body into losing fat, and anyway, what working mom has an hour every day to work out? Instead, do intervals of your cardio of choice (biking, walking, running, swimming) several times per week and lift heavy weights at least twice per week. We're not talking five-pound dumbbells here; we're talking big weights for compound movements (using two muscle groups at the same time— so efficient!) to burn fat and build functional muscles (not "date night" muscles) to keep you moving as Father Time ticks on.

DON'T GET DERAILED BY LOGISTICS

Ringmasters, none of you has time to hit thrice-weekly Pilates classes in your favorite studio across town. You're working serious hours at the office, and your second shift is no joke. But that's no excuse to skip workouts. In addition to scheduling time (and holding that time sacred!) on your calendar, you will have to get creative with getting your movement in. Here are strategies to make sure you move your body every single day, even when you can't make your favorite class.

FREE ONLINE CONTENT

Even if you're not a cord-cutter, you likely have some sort of video content subscription. There are literally thousands of hours of free fitness videos on Amazon Prime, Hulu, and Netflix. And if you're living under a rock and don't have one of those subscriptions, try YouTube. Can't (or don't want to) go to a gym? No problem. Search "women's body weight workout." Not sure how to start a weight-lifting regimen? Pull any weights video and watch the pros. My two favorites right now are YogaWithAdriene.com and HASFit. com for weights and bodyweight workouts.

TINY HOME GYM

I gave up my gym membership nearly a decade ago when I realized I just wasn't getting there and felt guilty about my membership dollars going to waste. I set up a small home gym, and so can you. There's a device (TV, laptop or phone) for video workouts. I keep a few sets of dumbbells and one kettle bell, resistance bands, and a "slider" (though you can use a plastic plate). With these at home, there's no excuse for not getting in some resistance training every week.

OFFICE WORKOUT

Sometimes, you just get chained to your desk. I blame face-time culture and the disheartening trend of "meetings that could have been emails." But fear not; you can move through the day. It sounds ridiculous, but every hour, I aim for draining my sixteen-ounce water bottle and a long trip to the ladies' room to get some steps. I take the stairs every chance possible (goodbye pumps, hello flats!) and propose "walking meetings" whenever I think my counterpart is game. If you can close the door to your conference room, office, or phone booth, try squats, lunges, and even wall push-ups while on endless conference calls. You are a grown-ass woman, and you don't care if you look ridiculous doing it so long as you get the movement your body needs in a jam-packed workday.

WORK OUT DURING KIDS' ACTIVITIES

Despite all of the scheduling paring you'll learn about in the next chapter, odds are you will spend your non-work evening and weekend hours shuttling your children to and from various activities. Rather than sitting in your car answering work emails on your phone, throw in a change of clothes to run laps around your eight year-old's soccer practice field. Keep a pair of sneakers in your car so that you can power walk in the trendy neighborhood where your son's guitar lessons take place, listening to a great podcast or audiobook. Sure, you could edit that document due tomorrow or cram in a few errands, but make this time about you.

ON BUSINESS TRAVEL

One of my secret mom confessions is that I really like occasional business travel. It's the only occasion when my time is fully "my time." Sure, you've got flights to catch and meetings to attend, but without ballet carpool in the evening or getting three wee beasties up for school, you can really make time for your workouts. Book a hotel that has a substantial gym, or if you're a swimmer, seek out one with a pool. Ask the concierge for recommendations of a nearby Pilates studio, as this may be the only time you can get that full hour-long class in. A friend who traveled weekly for business booked hotels one or two miles from her meeting sites and skipped the rental car nonsense so she could get walks in by necessity.

STRESS MANAGEMENT, NUTRITION, AND FITNESS FOR WORKING MOMS

Despite a reasonably healthy lifestyle, I had become frustrated with diminished returns on my exercise routine. I wasn't sleeping well, I was hungry (okay, hangry) most of the time, and the scale was creeping upward. Through my network (important in life, not just at the office!), I came to know Leslie Ann Quillen of FatLossLifestyleSchool.com, a personal trainer and nutrition coach for women. She helped me to switch up my workouts and meal plans so that I was fuller, happier, and less stressed. Turns out, stress is at the center of it all. With her help—and my sabbatical to write this book—in my last physical, my cholesterol was down 60 points, my blood pressure was at a steady rate, and the scale is at a steady spot I'm happy with.

Her approach aligns well with the Ringmaster framework; it's not that hard, you know what you need to do for you, and I give you permission to do it. Don't listen to the noise. Focus on you, reduce stress, eat well, and move your body, and you can kill it both at home and at the office.

HOW CAN CRAZY BUSY WORKING MOMS FIT EXERCISE INTO THEIR SCHEDULES? DON'T SAY TWICE-WEEKLY PILATES CLASSES—AIN'T NOBODY GOT TIME FOR THAT (BUT DAMN, WE WISH WE DID).

The first piece is movement. Our bodies are designed to move, and we have very sedentary lifestyles. Just start walking. For actual workouts, you do not need an entire hour at the gym to get an effective workout. Build your own tiny gym in your house or apartment with some dumbbells, kettlebells, bands, and a yoga mat. Focus on compound movements that work multiple big muscles at the same once. For example, squats, deadlifts, push-ups, rows, and overhead presses. Start with a twenty-to-twenty-five-minute strength training circuit twice a week, and you will see and feel a difference. You don't need to be in the gym one or more hours, six days per week, to feel changes in your body. Prioritize resistance training over cardio, and challenge yourself! Lifting weights and training intensely creates an "afterburn" effect: your body will continue to burn calories at an elevated rate for the next twelve to twenty-four hours. That doesn't happen with cardio. Another reason *not* to do hours of cardio? You will be a bottomless pit of hunger. Too much of the wrong kind of exercise impacts hunger hormones like ghrelin, which sounds a lot like *gremlin!* When ghrelin is elevated, you will not come home and make a nice salad. You're going to rip open the pantry and throw Goldfish crackers down the gullet. It's a vicious cycle of exercising more and eating more.

YOU ADVOCATE FOR WALKING TO MANAGE STRESS. WHY?

Kids, spouses, and work don't go away. You can't just put your head in the sand; there will always be stress! I think people feel powerless when trainers or doctors say, "You must handle stress." It's like, "But how do I do that? I'm stressed all day every day!"

We can all be proactive in stress management, and it's really simple to do. Walking lowers stress hormones like cortisol—especially if you walk outside. Most of us are in fight-or-flight mode all day long, feeling like we're running from danger. To activate your "rest and digest" system, take time for restorative yoga and practice deep breathing exercises. Lie on the floor and close your eyes. Put your hand on your belly and breathe in deeply, making your belly go up and down, for five to ten minutes. Your mind and body will relax.

WHAT'S THE CONNECTION BETWEEN DIGESTION AND STRESS?

I believe chronic stress is what's driving the majority of problems most women face every day. Ignore the stress, and it manifests in other ways. So many women come to me saying, "I'm bloated all the time. I think I might have irritable bowel syndrome or a food allergy." Another thing I hear a lot is, "My metabolism is broken."

That may be the case, but let's rule out the obvious stuff first, like stress. If you get your stress levels down and you are still dealing with digestive issues or other health concerns, then absolutely see a doctor (i.e. an allergist or gastroenterologist).

In a sympathetic state, your autonomic nervous system prepares the body to react to stresses, such as threat or injury. It causes muscles to contract and heart rate to increase, and digestion is not a priority if your body thinks it's in danger. Blood flow goes to big muscles like your arms and legs so you can run from tigers, or your cranky two-year old or demanding boss. And your lunch is just sitting in the gut, not moving, and you're feeling bloated—not to mention the fact that you wolfed it down while barely chewing. Slowing down and learning to manage stress can really help digestion!

HOW DO WOMEN WHO COMMUTE AND SIT IN AN OFFICE ALL DAY GET THEIR STEPS IN?

You have to get creative and just find the time. A lot of companies are open to flexible work schedules. If you can move your schedule outside of rush hour, you may just find that missing magic time. It's worth having a conversation about the implications on your health. "I love my job, but I want to maximize my time and energy. Can I work from home one day a week or stagger my schedule? Can meetings be online vs butt in a chair for eight hours a day to be productive?"

If you're good at what you do, if you're adding value, they're going to make things happen to keep you happy and productive. And wellness initiatives lower health insurance costs, a growing expense for most organizations. Be innovative. Let's be leaders. If you see a problem, speak up and offer a solution. The worst the boss can say is no.

WHAT ARE SOME OF THE BIGGEST MISTAKES WOMEN MAKE WHEN IT COMES TO NUTRITION?

The number one thing women tend to struggle with most is eating enough protein. They don't want to hear it, but it's true. Granola bars and fruit smoothies aren't the solution.

So much of the foods that are marketed to women as "high protein" are nothing more than cute packaging. Women's fitness magazines tell them to eat more nuts and beans and grains—foods that have some protein in them, but are much higher in fats and carbs respectively. For example, peanut butter is a fat, not a protein. Beans are not a protein; they are primarily a carbohydrate. The best sources of protein have little to no fat or carbohydrates. They are things like chicken, turkey, lean cuts of steak, and fish. For vegetarians, eat more eggs or egg whites. Protein powder and Greek yogurt are good options too.

A big bowl of lentils with sweet potatoes and cranberries may make you feel "healthy"—but it's basically a carb bowl with very little protein.

It's not about going "low carb" or "no carb." It's about finding the right amount and type for you based on your goals.

If your goal is fat loss, you must be in a *slight* caloric deficit to lose fat, and it's not as much as most people think. If you are eating real, whole, nutrient-dense foods that you love, you will feel full and not be hungry. I don't count calories or macros, and I don't teach my clients to either. We eat real food. We move our bodies. We stay consistent with the big rocks—nutrition, movement, and stress management—and the results come in waves.

CHAPTER 12

BUILDING YOUR VILLAGE

If I've learned anything in the last seventeen years of the working motherhood circus, it is this: You shouldn't have to do it alone. The highs, the lows, the pain and joy, it's all meant to be shared. To build your personal village, you have to find your people and commit to building those relationships. Your village is your support system—at home and at work—that you can call upon when one of those plates you're spinning inevitably crashes.

The village is even more important for single parents and those with less-than-equal partners in sharing the load. Despite all best efforts in Ring 2 (Life), you will get a sick kid call, and it will probably happen when you're walking into a major client meeting. Someone in your village at home will need to pick up said sick child, or someone in your village at work will need to step in and give that pitch.

And don't make the mistake of narrowly defining your village. It's not only for backup care; as your kids get older, the village becomes important as extra sets of "eyeballs" on your children as they grow up and become more independent. Last year, I was working from home, holding forth on a conference call, when I received a text from another mom that "the long-haired twin" was spotted leaving the high school campus for lunch against school rules. I switched my conference call to a Bluetooth headset, hopped in my minivan, and busted him personally, and took delight in it. I then sent a paragraphs-long text to this mom, thanking her for helping me to raise my children and keep them safe.

And again, more than backup daycare or extra eyeballs around the community, the village shares your physical and psychological burden. These are new and stressful times we are living in, and your village can help manage your sense of being overwhelmed. As technology continues to evolve, you can't rely on personal experience as a blueprint for how to parent through or around it. Sure you can look to your own experiences about curfews and when it's okay to date or walk to school alone, but you can't speak to social media appropriateness or cyberbullying from your childhood experience. It's a scary new world, and you need all the help you can get. You will need extra virtual eyes on Instagram feeds as well as around the neighborhood.

I live and breathe by my "Hood Moms" group text. It's how I hear firsthand about the latest lockdown at the elementary school or how the bus is running ten minutes late, and of course, the occasional bus stop happy hour. A quick text to this group gives me instant answers to a range of questions, from "What time does the school picnic start?" to "Does anyone have an extra lemon? Dinner is already on the stove and I'm short!"

I know that you understand the importance of the village, but our current social structure (often living far from family and support) doesn't support traditional villages. In this chapter, I will share several strategies for finding and building your own village. I hope that one or two of these ideas will resonate with you and that you will feel motivated, energized, and confident enough to reach out and build relationships with people who can help you be the best Ringmaster you can be.

We moved to our home when our twins were six months old. The first few months, over a long, dark winter full of ear and respiratory infections as I navigated a new job, were miserable and lonely. Between work, commuting, and mothering newborns, I was having a hard time finding time to meet up with my friends who were scattered across the D.C. metro area, up to an hour away. I needed to make some friends closer to home.

Parenthood can be extremely isolating at a time when you need support the most.

That spring, energized by cherry blossoms and warmer temperatures, I decided to throw the twins an epic first birthday party. We made it a *Survivor* theme and invited all of our friends and family who had helped us survive a year that included preemie twins, MBA graduation, a new house, a new nanny, and a new job. We took this epic party as an opportunity to reach out to our neighbors who we hoped would become new friends. My husband and I made flyers ("Change 'em! Feed 'em! Survivor!") and personally invited every single neighbor in person to attend our party, featuring twin kegs! Our elderly Korean neighbor turned up with a tray of egg rolls, and neighbors who had previously not met or socialized despite living on the same street for years became friends.

The reality is that once you become a parent, your mobility is restricted. It's not as easy to hop in your car after work and drive across town for drinks. Nap schedules and early bedtimes will mean your free time keeps you closer to home. Parenthood can be extremely isolating at a time when you need support the most. Enter neighbors as friends. You should know at least 50 percent of your neighbors and find a way to get to know them that resonates with you. You don't need to be best friends, but you should know who they are. Whether it's someone to make a bus stop pickup when you're running late or someone with whom you can share a chat over the fence when you're doing yard work after the kids go to bed (because that's the only time you can squeeze it in!), the tight neighborhood village has become a thing of the past. Here are some ideas of how to build this on your own.

NAMES

It may seem awkward if you've passed the same guy for years while walking your dogs, but stop him and say, "You know, it's weird—I've known your face for years but never asked you your name. Hi, I'm Jenn." And as soon as he walks away, whip out your smartphone and enter his name in Contacts. The next time you see "John with the gray labradoodle," greet him by name. I guarantee the conversation—and relationship—will grow from there.

BLOCK PARTY

Pick a block, or just a few houses, and host a front-yard or porch party. Do it outside when the weather is nice to minimize your prep—and cleanup work—and make it a potluck. One of my neighbors hosts a last-day-of-school popsicle party, while another hosts the pre-trick-or-treating hot cider front yard picnic for Halloween. Text or email invitations, or even better, ask in person. If a neighbor arrives and you don't have his or her contact information, get it then! "Karen, I don't think I have your phone number. Do you mind if I get it and add it to my 'bus stop group text' list?" Once you have the proverbial digits, it's easy to text a quick "Hey, I'm having a post-bedtime glass of wine on the front stoop—care to join me?"

FRONT YARD

If a block party is out of your comfort zone or feels like too much of a lift on your busy to-do list, take inspiration from this successful

village-building movement. Kristin Schell of TheTurquoiseTable.
com is on a mission to love her neighbors and make communities
of "front yard people." Ringmaster, by now you've been a rock star
at work and negotiated a 4:30 p.m. departure. You've eaten your
preplanned family dinner, and your husband—as part of your load-
sharing agreement—is on kitchen cleanup duty. Take your kids to
the front yard or sidewalk and pass the soccer ball. Greet commuters
coming home. Wave to the folks on an evening run or dog walk.
Put yourself out there. Start a conversation. Ask their names. Build
your village.

Just because you are building your local village doesn't mean you
need to neglect your friends farther away! Be it across town, on a
different schedule, or across the world, you can keep up with them.
Technology has driven us apart with less time for in-person contact,
but it can also be a joy. WhatsApp chats, regular facetime dates, you
name it. Leverage technology to stay in touch with your dearest, even
when they are no longer your "nearest." Plan a Sunday morning park
meetup in a neutral spot for a power walk or family playtime. Get a
girls' weekend with your college roommates on the calendar. These
are still your people, and you need them.

And at the end of the day, the village is about building and investing
social capital. As we learned in chapter 9, "Sharing the Load," much
like you don't want to keep score with your partner on whose turn it
is to make the bed, you don't want to keep score in the village. Rather,
you want to help others proactively to build up your social capital for
when you inevitably need it. I know your to-do list is full and your
day is packed, Ringmaster, but I promise you this: you will need to
call in some favors. Here are some ideas on how you can lighten the
load for your fellow Ringmasters, buying you some social capital you
will need to cash in at some point, likely sooner than later.

SNOW DAYS

If you (or your spouse) are planning to stay home for a school delay or cancellation, why not invite the neighbor kids over? They can entertain themselves so you can dial into work for a bit, and the next time school is cancelled because it *might* snow and you need to head out of town on business travel, you won't feel even a little bit bad about saying, "Hey, can anyone take Tommy today?"

DOUBLED MEALS

Has your neighbor's husband been on travel all week? Why don't you double one of your meals and drop it off? It takes you about two minutes longer to make a second meatloaf, and saving meal prep for your fellow Ringmaster at the end of a long solo-parenting week will pay dividends.

SICK DAYS

Notice your neighbor's sweet daughter wasn't at the bus stop again due to a recurring ear infection? It's not contagious, and you're working from home today anyway; why not invite her to hang out with her iPad on your couch so mom can go into work?

SIGN-UPS AND PICKUPS

Unless specified, you don't all have to stand in line for religious education sign-ups or camp registration. Give your fellow Ringmaster an hour back in her jam-packed day by standing in line for pre-ordered school supply pick-ups.

This all may sound a little hokey, but I am here to tell you that it works. Two years ago, I had a major abdominal surgery, a repair from my five-foot-one-inch frame carrying twins. I put off this surgery for years, as I knew it would take me out of my game for at least two months. But this is where seventeen years of village building came to fruition. All of the last-minute child coverage, bus stop pickups, and meal deliveries I did years earlier resulted in near-round-the-clock home care from two nurses, a month of dinner deliveries, and rides and walks to school for my youngest son while I recovered. I could not have done this without my village, and I am so grateful to each and every one of them.

CHAPTER 13

MANAGING THE STRESS

Ringmasters, by now you have built skills in managing the chaos of your working motherhood circus. You know how to prioritize and are confident about what goes into each of your rings. You are in control of when and where the spotlight shines. But the reality is, there will always be stress. Your spouse, your work, your children—they don't ever stop demanding your time or attention. And of course, you wouldn't want it any other way, but it is *hard*. This period you're in right now is the most intense part of your life. Just as you're trying to raise small humans, you hit the meatiest part of your career development curve.

But even with the best stress management strategy, the Ringmaster can crash. I should know; it happened to me.

It had been building for a while. The tension. The tears. The yelling. The sleeplessness. Uncertainty in the present and angst about the future. Work hell during the holidays met an unfortunately rough hormonal cycle, and I found myself awake all night on December 26, Googling symptoms for nervous breakdown. By my own self-diagnosis, I was four-for-seven and headed downhill.

I am a so-called expert on and lifelong student of work-life integration, and I was losing my shit. I mean, I was writing a book on this topic, and I couldn't calm my brain enough at night to sleep more than a few hours at a time. I hate the nickname "Wonder Woman," but I found a lot of my identity in my ability to do it all, even when things got tough. I can usually handle work when there is strife on the home front and can likewise weather professional storms when everything at home is going smoothly. When both are coming off the rails? Apparently, that's when Wonder Woman falls apart.

It had been a very tough work year for a lot of people, including me. The political tension that all Americans felt hit home directly, as the bulk of my business is in the federal sector. I led a very large, long-shot proposal, and—gulp—we won. But what was great news for the firm was not great news for me personally. A new role (and not one I particularly wanted) plus my regular day job duties and one helluva lot of uncertainty caused me to have heart palpitations while on the Metro platform on my morning commute, tears on my way out of the office most days, and complete mental and physical exhaustion when I arrived home each night. The kicker? Feedback from my bosses at my year-end review that I "look angry and frustrated all the time." Never mind the vaguely sexist undertone—they were right; I was angry and frustrated all the time.

At home, despite my best holiday management strategies, it was much of the normal chaos of a household with three boys and two full-time working parents. But now add in the stress of two teenagers who can't seem to manage their way out of a wet paper bag, whose grades were failing and who were testing limits, and the tension factor was high. Kid number three, content to hide out from the fray, was spending way too much time in virtual worlds. There was yelling. Lots of yelling.

And through all of this, I was painfully missing my best friend, who passed away three years ago. The one with the twins a day younger than mine, who was my boss during my MBA internship all those years ago and knew me so well she could call me on my BS and right my ship with one phone call. But she was gone, and I was going to have to figure this out on my own.

It's nine months later, and while I wouldn't say I am in the clear yet, things are looking up. I have given myself permission to nearly fall apart and the space to put myself back together. How did I do this? By going back to the basics. None of these ideas is earth-shattering, but if you are teetering on the edge, one or two of these things might work for you:

MOVE THE BODY/CALM THE MIND

For the last year, I have resisted the mat. I don't want to go to yoga or sit still for meditation, but I've made myself do it. I switched meditation apps for a new voice and made a daily challenge with a friend for accountability. My current favorite apps are Calm and Headspace. If I can't find the time in my day, I use my Metro commute for the meditation. And before bed, I put one hand on my chest and the other one my belly and breathe in deeply, exhaling one bit longer than the inhalation. I switched out long, time-consuming runs for shorter sprint workouts or heavy weights to make me feel strong. After a brisk walk to the office, I pause at the front door, taking three long breaths and setting an intention for the day.

PRIORITIZE SLEEP

After trying all of the normal things (lavender in the diffuser, "sleep stories" on Calm app, etc.), I finally called a family meeting and said that mom was going to need more sleep or life was going to suck for everyone. No teenagers banging around at midnight, no errant 3:00 a.m. alarms, no TV shows with my husband or the boys. Sleep above all else. I think that my behavior had been so crazy of late that they actually complied. And sleep begets sleep. The more you get, the easier it comes. And with more sleep, you have more patience for the little bosses at home and the nonsense at work. You have greater resilience to ride the emotional highs and lows that come along with running this circus.

SURROUNDINGS

Do whatever you have in your control to change your surroundings. Play mood-changing music. Hang out with positive, supportive people and limit your exposure to those who are not. Rearrange your work space. Buy yourself some flowers for home *and* work, and put some invigorating orange in your diffuser. When you're feeling the downward pull of the vortex, you need to change what you can so that you don't get sucked in.

GRATITUDE

I have never been able to keep an Oprah-style gratitude journal, or any journal, for that matter. It always felt like more work, one more thing on my to-do list. But when I would lie awake at night and worry about all the things, I would say to myself, out loud: "Warm bed. Dry roof. Healthy family. Loving friends." Sometimes you just need to remind yourself that these are first-world problems and that you are blessed beyond belief and stronger than you know.

SABBATICAL

I had been working on this book for nearly two years but could never get past the proposal phase. Despite a strong time management game, I couldn't find even thirty minutes a day to pursue this passion project. And even if I had, there wasn't an ounce of creativity left in me. I was emotionally and physically exhausted. I never took maternity leaves, as my twins were born when I was in graduate school and my third when I ran a start-up. So I put in for and was granted a four-month leave of absence so that I could write this book, spend the time with my family we all needed, and hit the professional reset button. Within a week, my blood pressure was down and I was sleeping through the night again.

A sabbatical, or any significant time off work, isn't an option for most people. It's terribly uncommon in the corporate world (though it shouldn't be!), but my break from work was made possible by years of hitting it out of the park. Of, year after year, adding significant and measurable value to my firm. In many ways, every word in the "Ring 1: Work" section is about teaching you how to kill it at work so that you can one day earn the benefit of taking a sabbatical, a break to work on a passion project or travel or hit the reset button.

And in "Ring 2: Life," I hope you've learned strategies and tips for managing the chaos of daily caregiving and running a household. Because they're right: the days are long, but the years are short. As my older two begin their senior year of high school, I am keenly aware of just how fast this time with them has gone. And no, I have no regrets about leaving the laundry till the next day or saying no to BS school or social activities that didn't work for our family.

But Ring 3, Ringmaster—that's about you. In reading this book, I hope that you never hit the level of burnout I felt. I didn't get quite there, but I was standing at the precipice, and it was scary. Because we are all living longer and basic necessities like health care and housing are getting more expensive, we are all likely to work a very long time in some form or fashion. And as it turns out, we are going to parent forever. This isn't a problem you can solve in the short term. There isn't some magic work schedule or daycare solution that will right your ship. This is a mindset. And you, Ringmaster, are in control. You are in charge of the beautiful circus you've created, and you will do great things. Godspeed.

EPILOGUE

THE FOLSOM HOUSE RULES

And lest you get to the end of this book thinking that I have it all figured out, I do not. My life is not Insta-perfect, and as it turns out, three *is* the magic number when it comes to the chaos created in a house of boys. As a mother to nearly eighteen-year-old twins and a twelve-year-old Little Prince, things come out of my mouth every day that I can't believe I actually have to say.

Many years ago, we began to jot them down on a list on the fridge, and the Folsom House Rules were born.

You'll notice a few themes here: personal safety, hygiene, and penises. When sharing the Folsom House Rules, I don't get the same reaction from friends with one boy. There's usually some nodding in agreement from moms of two boys, but all moms of three (or more!) boys just gently nod their heads and say, "Yep, I feel ya, sister." Mothers of girls? The response is outright horror.

The level of testosterone, energy, and destruction is something to behold. Every single day, I remind myself that I will miss the joyful noise when they're gone, but until then, a few rules to live by:

1. No hands in your pants when you're talking to Mom.

2. No wrestling while on crutches. Or in a cast. Or a boot.

3. If it touches your junk, don't put it where you eat.

4. You can dance, but you have to keep your pants on.

5. No cereal in your pockets.

6. Please keep grenades out of the kitchen.

7. In the shower, only touch your own penis.

8. No peeing off the deck or in the driveway.

9. No naked FaceTime.

10. Don't say "I'm hungry" with food in your mouth.

11. No safety cones on the dinner table.

12. No shooters in your bedroom.

13. When you find explosives, bring them to Dad.

14. No tooting in Mom and Dad's tent.

15. Don't pee in the bathroom trash can.

16. No biking in a hurricane (Sandy).

17. Keep the slap band bracelets off your neck and penis. And your brother's penis.

18. Don't pogo stick near the firepit.

19. No eating when you're on the phone.

20. Don't put grapes up your nose or in your eyes.

21. No dancing in an open sunroof while the car is moving.

22. It's a headlamp, not a penislamp.

23. No boomerangs in the house.

24. It's "Yes, ma'am," not "Gotcha, dog."

25. No naked Friday Night Movie Night.

26. One child at a time on the pull-up bar.

27. Don't leave whiskey, wine, liquor, or "any of that stuff" in the bathroom.

28. Big brothers lead by example.

29. No roughhousing with toothpicks.

30. If it's below freezing, you may wear shorts, but you may not complain about being cold.

31. No laptops where butts and feet go.

32. No teaching little brother to curse in other languages.

33. No crop-dusting in roller coaster lines.

34. Once it goes in your mouth, it doesn't come back out.

35. No dirty socks on the kitchen counter.

36. No loose candy lying around.

37. Don't jump off the stairs from more than three stairs up.

38. No peeing off the deck from *inside* the house.

39. Keep the condoms, surf wax, skateboarding tools, bike kit, and dirty socks off the table.

40. No backflips off of the deck railing.

41. You must shower daily. No, the pool/river/bay do not count.

42. Only one at a time on the roof and with Dad nearby.

43. Deodorant is a requirement, not a suggestion.

What will number 44 be? Your guess is as good as mine.